"PLAY IT WI

MW00895464

How to Win at the Game of Life
with the Rules of Golf

Don E. Peavy, Sr.

Hamilton Books
A member of
The Rowman & Littlefield Publishing Group
Lanham · Boulder · New York · Toronto · Plymouth, UK

Copyright © 2008 by
Hamilton Books
4501 Forbes Boulevard
Suite 200
Lanham, Maryland 20706
Hamilton Books Acquisitions Department (301) 459-3366

Estover Road
Plymouth PL6 7PY
United Kingdom

Library of Congress Control Number: 2007931801
ISBN-13: 978-0-7618-3823-4 (paperback : alk. paper)
ISBN-10: 0-7618-3823-6 (paperback : alk. paper)

To Juan Reyna and Maria Blanca Rangel de Tyson

Who taught me how to "Play It Where It Lies."

ಬಾಂ

CONTENTS

ACKNOWLEDGMENTS

U nless otherwise noted, all of the rules of golf cited in this work are taken from the book, *Golf Rules Plain & Simple*, by Mark Russell with John Andrisani. New York: HarperCollins Publishers, Inc., 1999. I will note specific references to this remarkable work by parenthetical page citations.

I am eternally grateful to Mike Mello, professor of English, Victor Valley College, for his counsel and editorial assistance in the preparation of this manuscript.

Don E. Peavy, Sr., Ph.D.

INTRODUCTION

My friends, to whom I have entrusted this manuscript for their advice and counsel, have been unanimous in asking me, "Why? Why a book of philosophy?" It seems as if they see something inimical in a pastor and theologian writing a book on philosophy—and practical philosophy at that.

The concern is expressed more profoundly by those who labored with me through graduate school, where I had no kind words for philosophy. There I said that not only was I not a philosopher, I saw no utility to the enterprise.

Then as now, I am convinced that philosophy has lost its way. Philosophy has become an academic endeavor that, as Macbeth lamented about life, is "full of sound and fury, signifying nothing." Philosophy has become the fodder for flights of fancy by academicians who, unable to respond coherently and constructively to the problems of this world, imagine another world where such problems do not arise. Such practitioners have reduced the language of philosophy to mathematical formulas, hypotheticals, and illogical syllogisms.

Oh, there are a few bright spots, such as D.Z. Phillips, but those are more the exception than the rule. For most people in North America, if not most parts of the world where television is readily available, philosophy has been reduced to the wisdom of Oprah and the pop musings of Dr. Phil.[1] Hardly anyone reads the ancient masters anymore, except for students who appropriate those works without understanding them or they are not able to translate this ancient wisdom into a wholesome and beneficial life.

The "cool place," of which Wittgenstein wrote, has become a cold and lifeless place. People cry out for an escape from their darkness and agony; yet, philosophy's only response is inaudible and unintelligible. That is because philosophers talk to each other and not to the people. Lost in translation between the ideal of philosophy and philosophy as it lies still-born in the womb of the academy is the transformative power of philosophy.

Philosophy became the enterprise of the enlightened not because it was "cool," but because it could transform one's life from the mundane to the enriched. Philosophy was not some pie in the sky; it was the bread and butter of a good life right here on earth. To that extent, it was, as Weber has said of nascent religion, "economic." Philosophy did not, as theology was to do much later and continues to do today, call people to live a life that would ensure their good fortune in the life to come (although, as Plato dreamed in "The Republic," such a life could result in one's eventual return to the Monad); philosophy called people to live a life worthy of enlightened creatures that affords them the best possible life in this world without any "carrot" being dangled before them. Philosophy sought to transform people—not to bribe them or to threaten them.

Consider the following account which has been preserved for our edification by Prophry and reported to us by Robert Louis Wilken:

> There was also Rogatianus, a senator, who advanced so far in renunciation of public life that he gave up all his property, dismissed all his servants, and resigned his rank. When he was on the point of appearing in public as praetor and the lectors were already there, he refused to appear to have anything to do with the office. He would not even keep his own house to live in, but went the round of his friends and acquaintances, dining at one house and sleeping at another (but he only ate every other day). As a result of this renunciation and indifference to the needs of life, though he had been so gouty that he had not been able to stretch out his hands, he became able to use them much more easily than professional handicraftsmen. Plotinus regarded him with great favor and praised him highly and frequently held him up as an example to all who practiced philosophy.[2]

Notice that the transformation of the senator occurs not because he fears damnation or because he seeks eternal life beyond the present state of affairs. The senator's change is brought about merely at the instance of his need to seize a more quality life than the one he is living. And more importantly, the change comes about due to the senator's own efforts and his submission to the wisdom of his teacher. Rogatianus' transformation is the result of his willingness to practice philosophy and not just meditate upon it. This is the power of philosophy. This is the epitome of practical philosophy.

Philosophy's power of transformation is not limited to individuals. It can alter the course of institutions and movements as well. Christianity was but a provincial religion before the Apostle Paul infused it with Greek philosophical ideals and in so doing projected this nascent faith into the forefront of religions that would lead to its being adopted as the official religion of the Roman Empire—the same entity that once persecuted it. Likewise, Islam had taken its place at the table of the West and was quite content to be just one of the many until Sayyid Qutb's philosophy enflamed it and caused it to exert itself on the world's stage and to transform nations and institutions into the image of what he perceived Islam demanded.[3]

I contend that in losing its way, philosophy has lost this transformative element and with it the light it once offered to those marooned in the dark woods. If these things be true, then why philosophy and not theology or religion? Again, I hear the pleas of my friends. Why have I chosen to write philosophy and not theology or religion? I have chosen philosophy or rather it has chosen me because despite its present morass, philosophy stands a much better chance of being revived and reaching the mass of people than does the exclusiveness of theology or the divisiveness of religion.

With due honor and respect to thinkers such as Hick, Cobb, Wilfred Cantrell Smith, and others who have written valiantly about global theology and a world religion, I am convinced that such ideas are but noble fancies. It may be that Panikkar is quite right when he says that religious diversity is the work of God as exemplified by the myth of the Tower of Babel. Any attempt by humans to undo what

God has done is idolatrous and blasphemous and doomed to failure. In recognition of Panikkar's wisdom, I have set forth here a path that opens up to people of all religious traditions.

If there is to be a way of life accessible to all peoples, then philosophy offers the best hope for the construction of such a road, and that is the reason that I have turned to philosophy for the presentation of a way of life that is universal in its application. No matter what a person's ultimate destiny might be, the road presented here will make the journey a great deal easier and significantly more fulfilling.

Though I have not taken a survey of people everywhere, I think it is safe to say that all people seek to live life to its fullest and with the least degree of pain. Even the sadist and the masochist seek moments of repose when they can be silent and at peace. This universally shared quest for life offers a foundation on which a philosophy of life can be constructed. That is the task of this book. Whether I have succeeded or failed—others will have to decide. As for me, I take comfort in knowing that I have tried.

1

PLAY IT WHERE IT LIES

During my first year of undergraduate studies, a friend of mine, Juan Reyna, consented to instruct me in the game of golf. He reasoned that if I were going to move into the ranks of the middle class upon graduation, I had to take on another past time other than bowling. And so off to the golf course we went where I purchased a pair of shoes and rented a set of clubs and irons. Juan was kind enough to bring along a requisite supply of golf balls as well as his own bag, shoes and all the other accouterments of the sport. I complained about the cost of this new sport. "It's an investment in your future," Juan counseled. "You'd be surprised how many fortunes are won and lost on golf courses," he advised, as he placed his hand gently on my back to reassure me that I had ventured upon the right path. Little did he know that the game of golf would, in fact, affect my future. Not in an economic way, but most profoundly in a spiritual one as I came to understand an approach to life that parallels how one plays the game of golf.

Rule Number 1

"Play It Where It Lies"

Juan guided me every step along the way in this my first foray into the game of golf. However, he could not stroke the ball for me. Though I wished he could have. It took me 12 strokes to finally get my ball to fall into the cup of the par four first hole. Juan had to remind me that, in golf, the object is to get the lowest score and not the highest as is the case in bowling. After my second tee off, my ball went into the rough and lodged against a tree. I bent down to move my ball to a more preferred position when Juan shouted, "Play it where it lies!" He explained to me that was the fundamental law of the game of golf, and that I could not "willy nilly" move my ball around. If I could not play the ball where it lay then I faced five possibilities:

1. I could fudge the ball along until it's in a better position (as I was attempting to do) but this would be cheating;

2. I could hit the ball where it lies;

3. I could pick the ball up and drop it at a point "where the ball originally lay between the hole and the point where" I drop it and in doing so incur a penalty stroke;

4. I could say to hell with the game and leave, in which case I would forfeit the game, and others hearing about my action would refuse to play golf with me in the future;

5. I could do nothing, in which case he or someone else would make the decision for me, and this could mean my being ejected from not only the game but the golf course as well.

I considered each of these options. I figured I was already a number of strokes behind Juan and another stroke would put me further behind. Rather than take the penalty stroke, I decided to try to hit the ball soft enough to get it into the fairway then try to hit it hard enough to make up for the short distance. This was a strategy born more out of wishful thinking than reasoned analysis. The strategy I was mapping out depended on such skill that a great many seasoned professionals could not accomplish it. Nevertheless, at the time I was shocked to discover that my gentle stroke hardly moved the ball at all. And what was more disheartening, I was now another stroke behind Juan and would incur yet another one when I dropped the ball according to the rule.

I wanted to abandon my foray into golf and tell Juan the middle class would just have to get used to my bowling. But then, the words of my military basic training unit's motto invaded my mind: "A winner never quits and a quitter never wins." So on I pressed into what would be one of the most humiliating and humbling days of my life as well as one of the most instructive, although the lessons learned would take a number of years to coalesce in my psyche and to move from lessons learned to life lived.

Rule Number 2

Life Is A Game

I believe this rule of golf, "Play it where it lies," and the responses to it are an apt metaphor for playing the game of life. The *Random House Webster's Dictionary* defines game as "a competitive activity involving skill, chance, or endurance played according to rules." Life is a game in that it too is an activity (living) that has rules (our ethics, morals, mores, laws, values, etc.; rules of nature and physics), and a field of play (the world). Life is a competition in which we compete against the impulses and desires of our flesh and id as well as the powers of the world. Golf is a game in which one competes against oneself, external forces, and the forces of nature.

How well one has studied and practiced, whether one got a good night's sleep, whether one has chosen the proper equipment with which to play the game, and many other factors determine one's success in the game of golf. Likewise, the direction and strength of the wind, field conditions, crowd noise, and a myriad of other factors have to be reckoned with in one's approach to the game of golf. Interestingly, none of these factors have anything to do with one's playing partner. That is why in golf, the people with whom we play golf are called partners and not opponents. For one is playing against oneself and the external forces of nature and not other golfers. This is one of the salient gifts of the game of golf as well as the game of life—we can play and excel without having to gain an advantage over others. We can win without others having to lose.

In the game of life, though, unlike golf, there is no "cut" that insures that a predetermined number of players will not make it to the money winning stage. In the game of life, every player has an opportunity to end up in a place where he/she will receive some degree of payment. And although some players will end up with more money than other players, that is no cause for alarm. There is always another tour event. Likewise, those who don't make it to the top in this field of play can always look forward to the world to come where everyone is promised to be a winner for ever more. And even if there is no life beyond this life, one can take comfort in knowing that one has played it where it lies and one can take pride in having lived an authentic life and in having done the very best one could have done.

In this life however, where we end up is not as important as how we play the game. For despite all that we do, despite our training and plans and practices, we may achieve tragic results on the field of play due to no fault of our own. We can be struck by lightning even though there were no dark clouds to warn us. A stray ball can send us into darkness just as an out of control crowd can trample us underfoot. We have succeeded when and if we have lived a good, moral life in union with the ultimate reality, and, to paraphrase the words of Sir Elton John, life is made more wonderful by our having been in the world. This success can be achieved no matter the level of performance of others in the game. As said previously, we are not in competition with others. To succeed at this game of life, we have only to gain the advantage over internal and external forces.

The Apostle Paul spoke of the conflict within us when he said:

> For that which I do I allow not: for what I would, that do I not; but what I hate, that do I. If then I do that which I would not, I consent unto the law that it is good. Now then it is no more I that do it, but sin that dwelleth in me. For I know that in me (that is, in my flesh,) dwelleth no good thing: for to will is present with me; but how to perform that which is good I find not. For the good that I would I do not: but the evil which I would not, that I do ... But I see another law in my members, warring against the law of my mind, and bringing me into captivity to the law of sin which is in my members.[4]

Buddha also stressed this internal war, when he spoke of the Four Noble Truths, and how this war that rages inside of us can be won by following the Eight-fold Path. We find further explication of this internal conflict in the Koran, where the Prophet writes of the Jihad that goes on within the faithful as they fight against the evil desires of the flesh. This internal struggle is the "greater" jihad, whereas the jihad of which we in the West hear so much in the news is the "lesser" jihad. No doubt, it is much harder to tame the fires that rage within us than it is to control another person.

We turn again to Paul to enlighten us on the external competition as well:

> Put on the whole armour of God, that ye may be able to stand against the wiles of the devil. For we wrestle not against flesh and blood, but against principalities,

against powers, against the rulers of the darkness of
this world, against spiritual wickedness in high
places.[5]

Paul, Buddha, and the Koran agree that we are in competition not against others, but against ourselves. This competition is dramatized in the novel and movie, "Dr. Jekyll and Mr. Hyde." There is a Dr. Jekyll and Mr. Hyde in everyone, fighting for dominance and survival. The Mr. Hyde lurks in the murky waters of our id. Philosophy and religion seek to equip us with skills that can keep him at bay. Drugs and alcohol, as well as other stimulants, dissolve the wall that philosophy and religion have constructed and allow Mr. Hyde to emerge and wreak havoc in our lives. Our success in the game of life is determined in large part by how well we have kept Mr. Hyde confined to his prison in our id. The increasing accounts of road rage in North American culture may be a sign that we are losing this battle. Gang violence among our youth is evidence that a serious rupture has occurred in the psyche of our young people, and this crevice can only worsen as they become adults and give birth to children with genetically weakened structures of self-control. I doubt we can repair this breach by just saying no to its existence.

Life, then, is a game. If we are to be successful at this game, we must recognize and obey its rules. These rules are more than what we refer to as the laws of nature.[6] They are rules that are inculcated by religion and philosophy and by living in human society. There are far too many of these rules to make any attempt to list them here. Our task is to show simply how "play it where it lies" is the most fundamental of these rules. We are to live out our lives as they are in the field of play in which we are located. We cannot wish our lives to be other than what they are. We cannot wish ourselves to be at a place other than where we are. We have to abandon the ifs, the maybe's, the when's, and take full responsibility for making the right choices and living our lives fully in the now. We have no resort to a machine in which we can travel back in time to either correct past mistakes or project ourselves into an uncertain future to see how our choices will turn out. We have only today, and we must choose and accept the consequences of our choices.

Rule Number 3
Life Is A Given; How We Live Is Not

Playing it where it lies does not signify reckless abandon, nor does it mean that we cannot strive to reform ourselves and our environment. Rather, this path requires ongoing analysis, reflection, and reformation. Our project does however, demand that one recognizes one's "lie" in life and respond accordingly while complying with the rules of the game of life. For shortcuts often lead to long suffering. Much like Camus' Guest, when we attempt to circumvent the rules of the game, we go merrily down the road of destruction.

As I write these words, I am spending the Christmas and New Year's Eve holidays in Iloilo City, Philippines. Yesterday, I decided to partake of a transcultural[7] delight, so I visited a local McDonald's, where I ordered chicken and spaghetti. The meal came with only one piece of chicken, and I wanted two, so I asked the clerk to give me an extra piece of chicken. He said he could not. I clarified that I was willing to pay for the extra piece of meat. He responded that the meals could not be altered. I was about to launch into a barrage of "what's wrong with you people?" and other such "American" responses when I remembered the wisdom of this present work. I then ordered two meals.

I realized that I was not in America. I was in the Philippines. It will cause me untold problems and stress if I were to live my life as if I were still in America. I cannot expect people to change their rules and policies for me. The world does not revolve around me. We Americans need to face that reality and abandon our belief that our culture and way of doing things is the superior one. My stay in the Philippines was much better after I learned to "play it where it lies."

This is not to suggest that we cannot have dreams and aspirations and work to change those things that are oppressive, antiquated and the like. Quite the contrary. We can dream and we can plan and we can hope. But we must do so in such a manner that we do not squander the life we have while hoping for another one. I believe it was John Lennon who said that "Life is what happens while we're making plans." Too many of us spend our lives planning to live when some event occurs in the future. We will travel the world when we retire. We will return to school when our children grow up. We will do this, that or the other as soon as ... and the list goes on. As I put the final touches to this book, the Enron scandal continues to capture the headlines. Wrapped up in that sad tragedy are the countless lives ruined by the financial collapse of this giant corporation and the sudden reduction in value of its pension and 401K funds. So many people had been counting on those funds to provide the resources for the life they were planning to live one day in the unknown future. Now, those plans have evaporated into the mist of absurdity. People who were close to retirement now discover they will have to continue to work. "Life is what happens while we're making plans."

Of course, the opposite extreme of this living for tomorrow is the so-called "instant gratification" that plagues our young people and people not so young. Just as we can waste our lives by not living today, we can waste them by living as if there is no tomorrow. There is always a tomorrow whether or not we are alive to witness it. As the theme song from the movie "The Poseidon Adventure" reminds us, "There's got to be a morning after." Consequently, there should always be a balance between how I live and how I plan to live. One should always have a plan for living life beyond today, even as one lives as if today is all that one has. Actually, today is all that one has. And yet, there is always the possibility that one's game will last beyond the given. This is the mystery of the game we call life. It is a mystery that we can only appreciate. We can never pierce it successfully or fully understand it. Notwithstanding these limitations, we can enjoy life in the presence of mystery.

Our proposal here is toward that end. Life is a given. What we do with it is not. With all due respect to Sylvia Browne and Edgar Cayce, I am not persuaded by their arguments that we choose to come here to learn lessons that we could not learn on the "other side."

I do not think anyone chooses to come here. Even though many Christians proclaim that Jesus Christ chose to come into the world of space and time, at least the Gospel of John challenges that view. For at John 3:16, it is written that "God sent" Jesus Christ into the world. Further, the synoptic gospels and the Gospel of Thomas record the parable of the wicked husbandmen,[8] in which Jesus tells the story of a son who is sent by his father. Again, that story does not have the son choosing to go to the husbandmen. The son is sent by the father. Likewise, although the Buddha eventually realized that he was in Nirvana before his descent to earth, he could not remember making a conscious decision to undertake the journey, although he was sent here to lead us to enlightenment. Life, then, is a given. We have no say in where and when we will be born. This is our "lie" in the game of life. We do however, have control over how we respond to the life we are given.

It is a common error in human existence to presume there is a divine order to things, and that we enter life with a purpose and a plan. The enlightened Thoreau could saunter through nature and behold the grandeur of an order without any attention to the cataclysmic war raging within the ant kingdom or the muted cries of the insect writhing in terror on a web of deceit constructed by a spider who watches in bemused anticipation as its next meal tenderizes itself. Thoreau could behold the quietness of Walden Pond in total disregard to the battles for survival being waged beneath its surface. Likewise, cosmologists can peer out into the heavens and see a design of order and purposefulness without ever taking account of the many failed worlds and universes that have come and gone in order that those beheld by humans can exist. Hardly a minute goes by that another star does not go nova or a black hole emerges where beauty and light once were.

Thoreau and cosmologists are not alone in their failure to see neither "out far nor in deep." They presume an order that is not there. They opine a purpose and plan that is nonexistent. Likewise, many of us envision that our lives have a purpose that is written in the grand scheme of ultimate reality. Our lives have meaning that is defined by the "divine plan." And thus it is that when things go awry, we say in disgust, "Why did this happen to me?" We can ask such a question because we believe we are beyond such adversity, and that our lives have a greater purpose than to suffer and to fail. When "bad things" happen to us, we see this as an aberration of the divine order of things. Consequently, we are twice as afflicted because we are disturbed at the center of our being, trying to discern what it is we have done or not done to deserve such a fate.

At such moments of despair, we fail to see that what happens to us is not an aberration, but the way life is. There is no plan that guides our lives. Each of us must take responsibility to imbue our lives with meaning and purpose. We are not actors on a stage performing roles assigned to us by some cosmic director who has scripted a play with a definite beginning and ending. There is no such order to the universe. If there is to be meaning and purpose to our lives—then we must give them such. If we are to play the game of life successfully then we must make choices and accept the responsibility for the choices we make. We do this in full recognition that just as we are making choices, so are other people—either intentionally or by default—and these choices may lead to conflicts with our own. Then there are choices being made and not made by nature that may be in conflict with the choices we make, so that nature's tornado may conflict with our choice to construct a house at a certain place.

These factors mean that what happens to us in life is oftentimes beyond our control. How we respond to those happenings, however, is not. It is no wonder that we do not have abiding labels for other people's "lies" in the game of life. Oh, we say things such as he came from a broken home; she is an orphan, etc. However, these things do not mark out a path of behavior or a consciousness that such persons will always manifest. For every child we can name who was an orphan and whose life met with tragedy, we can name many more who accomplished significant and wonderful things in life. Charles Dickens, Lorenz Graham, and Horatio Algiers have left us with many testimonies of people whose lie in life did not dictate the content of their character or the outcome of their game. They have chronicled the lives of many who were able to play it where it lies and achieve great and wonderful things despite the challenges, and at times the overwhelming obstacles, presented by their lie.

Consequently, it is not in the lie that one's game is measured. It is in the response. This is a truth that many of my friends who profess to be Christians seem to struggle with. They profess a faith in a "God who is able," and yet the moment they fail to live a "perfect" life that God calls them to lead, they retreat behind the refrain, "I'm only

For later he declares that, "I can do all things through Christ which strengtheneth me."[9] As John the Elder declares, "Greater is he that is in you, than he that is in the world."[10] My Christian friends[11] seem to be unaware of these scriptures. They seize on the agony of Paul and, buttressed by the theology of Augustine, never get beyond what one historian has called "Christian mediocrity."[12] It is no wonder then that so many national leaders of Christianity become embroiled in scandals involving sexual and financial improprieties. These are they who say they do not have to play it where it lies because they are "just human." Yet, if humans cannot play it where it lies, who can? If humans cannot be imitators of Jesus Christ or the Buddha, then is not their coming into the world in vain? God forbid.

Humans can play it where it lies and pass what I like to call the hammer test. When I was a little boy, a friend and I were watching our pastor build an addition on to our church building. The pastor, noticing the intensity of our staring, turned to us and asked, "You boys interested in being carpenters?"

"No sir," responded my friend. "We are waiting to see what you say when you hit your finger with that hammer!"

Hitting his finger with the hammer would say nothing about the character of our pastor. Yet, how he responded would speak volumes. If he cursed, then it would be a sign his faith had not found a footing in his life—that his soul was not "anchored in the Lord." Jesus reminds us of this hammer test when he says, "There is nothing from without a man, that entering into him can defile him: but the things which come out of him, those are they that defile the man."[13] Hitting our finger with a hammer is a temporary lie. How we respond is our eternal being.

Of course, this volume makes no pretense to perfection, that is the task of religion. This volume will have succeeded if it merely lifts up a path that one can travel successfully in negotiating the game of life. In seeing how others have responded and the results of those responses, it is hoped that we can avoid repeating the mistakes of the past: that we might move into a brighter future while living a more meaningful present. This book is premised on the belief that part of what it means to be human is to possess remarkable creative energy. That energy can be marshaled in such a way that no matter where we lie in the course-way of life, we can excel even as we play it where it lies. And even where our lie is a tragic one, we can play out that tragedy with decency, courage, and fortitude. We can win even as we breathe out our last breath as the pantheon of heroes attests.

Rule Number 4

Live Life with Intentionality

Playing it where it lies requires us to live authentic lives with intentionality and to have a coach. By living an authentic life, I mean to recognize that if we are not religious, we are, as Moby reminds us, all "made of stars." We are children of the universe—emanations from that big bang that exploded into the vastness of space and existence. That creative process continues. There is no plan—just creative forces at play. We can and ought to participate in that process by helping to shape the form that creation takes. We can help calm the raging seas and the turbulent winds or channel those forces into more productive forms. We can assist in the distribution of resources so that all people everywhere will have the basic necessities that make for a dignified human existence in which no human ever goes to bed hungry involuntarily.

If we are religious then we need to harmonize our lives with the fact that we are created in the image and likeness of ultimate reality. Part of that ultimate reality is incarnated in us in the presence of the divine spark, our Buddha nature, our chakra, or our Krishna consciousness. We need to unify ourselves with that inner reality so that we may fully realize all that we are capable of doing and being. "Greater things shall" we do when we are connected to the vital source of our being that is incarnated within us. That promise is dramatized in the marvelous movie "Star Wars," in that pivotal scene where Luke Skywalker is attempting to destroy the Death Star. Luke needs to position his star fighter into a narrow corridor of the Death Star in order to launch a destructive missile. Luke continues to grapple with the controls of his ship, which gets increasingly more out of control. Then the voice of Obi One Kenobi invades the ship and counsels Luke to let go and let the Force take over. Luke, like so many of us humans feels he has to be in control. But later, he relents and lets go. The Force guides the ship into the narrow corridor, where Luke fires the missile that destroys the Death Star and saves the struggling colonies.

Like Luke, we too must realize the existence of the Force (whether we perceive it as being personal or impersonal) and harmonize our lives with it. It is then that we will discover that there are no races—only the human race. We are all brothers and sisters who hail from a common set of parents, whether they are cosmic forces or emanations from the plethora.

By intentionality is meant living life with eyes wide open. Think of all the people who have computers and mobile phones and who never get beyond the default settings. Those marvelous instruments would do so much more if people would spend the time reading the instruction manual and getting to know the machines. So it is with our lives. We need to intend that our lives have meaning and purpose. We need to read the instruction manuals for life that we might get all that we can. This book and other books, sacred scripture, classics from the ancient masters—all of these will help us to live more directed lives. A few years ago, I spent Christmas Eve with a group of Catholic friends. I was shocked to discover that not a single one of them knew the meaning of the Immaculate Conception. They were all life-long Catholics who had given their consent to a concept of which they knew little or nothing—a concept that is vital to their faith, as well as to the faith of all Christians. Like those Catholics who did not know the meaning of the Immaculate Conception, too many of us resign ourselves to let happen whatever will happen. We live our lives in the margins of default. We participate without getting involved. We listen without hearing. We squander this precious gift of life and forfeit our creative power because we do not read the instruction manuals that are available to us.

Living life with intentionality also means having a plan. There are many of us who have dreams and aspirations but no plan of accomplishing them. It is like the young man (whom we will meet later in this work) who was arrested for attempting to steal a Christmas tree. He knew Christmas was coming and that he would need a tree; however, he had no plan for fulfilling that need and so at the last moment he had to resort to criminal conduct. Not only do we not have a plan, many of us are engaged in conduct directly opposed to the realization of our dreams. I just discovered that a young student whom I helped to get a scholarship so she could finish school is pregnant. I asked her how did she expect to enroll in school the next semester when her baby is due within the next month or so, and she responded, "I don't know." She dreams of finishing school, yet she is engaged in conduct that directly keeps her from realizing that dream. And even if she does get to school, as so many others eventually do, think how much more complicated her mission is going to be with the responsibility of an infant. I do not know many golfers who intentionally hit their balls into sand traps. And yet, this is exactly what this young lady has done. Whether she did it intentionally or by default does not matter. The result is the same. I can only hope that she accepts the penalty and gets back in the game in a more positive and intentional way.

Rule Number 5
Get A Coach!

Additionally, one needs a coach. I was impressed some time ago when during a golf tournament Tiger Woods summoned his coach to help him to overcome problems he was experiencing. How many others would refuse to take such a step for fear of "wounding" their pride? Clearly, it is a sign of a pro who can call in help when help is needed. The young man who attempted to steal the Christmas tree needed help, but for whatever reason he refused to summon it. All of us need a coach—someone on whom we can depend to come to our aid in a time of trouble. It is refreshing to hear some people speak of their God with the words; He may not come when you want Him, but He is always on time!"

Of course, one's coach need not be a god or other cosmic power. One needs only to have someone to trust and upon whom one can depend to act as one's coach in the game of life. This person would typically be someone who has been there—that is, they have experienced various aspects of the game of life, and they have been relatively successful at it. A teacher or professor, a minister, a prayer partner or guru, a rabbi, or the coach of a sports team: all are potential candidates. Of course, there is no reason why one or both of one's parents could not fulfill this role. If a parent, then the parent must be willing to set aside what the parent hopes for the child in order to advise the child on the path the child has chosen. An older brother or sister can also fulfill the role of one's coach in the game of life.

Sometimes, even a good book can be an effective coach. The story is told about George Gershwin being commissioned to compose a piano concerto for which he would be the solo pianist. Gershwin had never written a piano concerto and thus was not familiar with the technical aspects of such an undertaking. However, Gershwin did not allow pride to get in his way. This great creative genius realized he needed a coach. He did not think himself too great or too smart to seek the advice and counsel of others. And so it was that Gershwin sought the advice of his friends and consulted a book on the orchestrations of a concerto. Those of us who appreciate classical music are forever grateful to Gershwin for the Piano Concerto in F that he gave us after consulting with his coach. Part of the uniqueness of Gershwin was he knew how to play it where it lies.

Keep in mind, though, that the best of coaches is ineffectual if we do not call them when we are in trouble and when we are not, for at times a coach can help us to avoid the unplayable lie as well as help us to negotiate it.

Finally, the Preacher reminds us that "There is no new thing under the sun."[14] This way of life that I expound on here is not new. It is already intimated in our language. We say things like: "Get real!" "Why doesn't she act her age?" "He ought to be ashamed of himself dressed like that." "They are living beyond their means." Sayings like these suggest that a person is not living according to the person's position in life—that the person is not playing it where it lies.

Thus, I am not offering something new. I am merely providing clarity to what is already adrift in the fog that covers the land. Like a midwife, I am but completing the work begun by others.

2

THE FUDGERS

W hen I attempted to fudge my ball along the way, I retreated to the first response to "Play it where it lies." Although I did not know I was violating a rule of golf, this does not lessen the magnitude of my offense. We have heard it said throughout the ages that "ignorance of the law is no excuse." That is because the law is based on common sense. The law demands no more than what common sense should tell us we ought to do or not do in any given situation. Consequently, I should have known that I could not just arbitrarily pick my ball up and move it wherever I pleased. This is also true of most people who break the law and violate the rules. They know that they are engaging in misconduct. The moment I attempted to fudge my ball along, I became a fudger. I am thankful that I had a friend who rescued me from this plunge into fudgery.

Our penal institutions are filled with fudgers. Our parole and probation departments are overwhelmed by them. These are the people who refuse to play it where it lies. They choose instead to cheat, to fudge their ball along the fairways of life when they think that no one is looking or that they can get away with it; or worst, they just don't care. These are the people who charge for work they have not done, who rob and steal, who pad the books, who lie, cheat, swindle and commit all manner of wrongs. We have become increasingly aware, thanks to continuous news services, that fudgers are not just the petty criminals we see on the cop shows and "the most stupid criminal" shows. There are fudgers in high places of government and in oak paneled corporate offices. There are even fudgers among the shepherds who think that God, like justice, is blind.

Rule Number 6

Don't Save Face by Losing at Life

Such people believe that either the rules of the game of life do not apply to them, or that their circumstances grant them an exemption from the rules—that one ought to obey the rules so long as it is convenient for one to do so. Take for instance, the plight of the uncle of a young girl—both of whose names have been lost to posterity.[15] The uncle was the trustee and guardian of his niece whom he raised without incident until she was nine years of age. Unfortunately, for the uncle, nine turned out to be a terrible number for him. For during that ninth year, he found it necessary to spare not the rod against his young ward who disappeared between the time of her punishment and the next day.

The weary uncle could not bear to face his neighbors and suffer the weight of the stares and comments that he imagined would come his way were his neighbors to discover that his ward had run away from home. For surely they would think him to be a monster of a guardian who had brought shame to the name of his late brother who had entrusted him with such an honorable task as administering his estate and caring for his daughter. Why else would so sweet and innocent a child have run away from home?

And so the uncle began to make excuses for the absence of his niece. When the neighbors grew tired of these excuses and went to the authorities, he concocted a scheme in which he hired a young girl to dress as his niece. Thus he was able to create a visage of being a good, kind and loving uncle. He was able to garner the admiration of his neighbors and to walk circumspectly in the world. He did not yet know that as the world giveth, the world taketh away. For soon his world was turned upside down and the blazing sun of absurdity pierced through the cloud of illusion he had created. Thus it was that he was revealed as a fudger.

His scheme was exposed and he was arrested for the murder of his niece. For who would go to such extreme measures to perpetrate a fraud except it be to cover up a hideous crime? And is not infanticide one of the most hideous of crimes? Thus it was that the uncle was arrested, indicted and tried for the murder of his niece.

At trial, the uncle tried to explain how he had devised the scheme because he feared the ridicule of the community if it knew his niece had run away from home. Nonsense, responded the prosecutor.

Children run away from home all the time. What is the need for us to resort to such a fraud? There could be no reason except to cover up the crime of murder. Furthermore, argued the prosecutor, if the uncle lied about his niece before his arrest, how could we be certain he is not lying about her now?

The prosecutor's question must have hit at the heart of the jury even as it punctured the balloon of hope that the uncle had launched about him. Surely, it points to the enigma fostered by those who lie. When a person tells a lie, how can we ever trust them to tell the truth? Once one starts tumbling down the slippery slope of lying, it is difficult if not impossible for one to ever regain one's footing! And so it was for the uncle. He was convicted of the murder of his niece and sentenced to be hanged. It was almost seven years to the date he was hanged that his niece returned to town.

Being hanged seems a rather harsh penalty to pay for lying. However, the uncle's crime is much more serious than mere lying. He was a fudger. He refused to play it where it lies. He chose instead to fudge his ball along the fairway of life, hoping that no one would see him doing so. Nevertheless, in a way, the uncle did murder his niece for he killed the sentiments which many bore of her. He slaughtered their hopes of ever seeing his niece again and caused untold suffering among those who must have mourned her killing. As a result of his crime, no one went looking for her or tied a yellow ribbon around an old oak tree to keep hope alive that one day she might return. The uncle had murdered her in the minds of the community—he had murdered her spirit even if her body continued to wander the earth. If Malidoma Patrice Somé is correct that there is a metaphysical universe in which our thoughts create beings that act out what is formed in our minds, then surely the uncle was guilty of murder.

Our wayward uncle made the mistake that so many of us make everyday of our lives—we presume that life ought to be other than what it is. He presumed that children ought to remain home with their parents or guardians, and that the community would look down upon him if his young ward did not do so. He believed wrongly that guardians exercised control over the passions of their wards. We cannot control our own hearts. How then can we control the hearts of others?

Yet, where is it written that children are to remain home until released by their parents? Is this not a presumption on our part? At best it is a hope and as a parent it is a hope to which I cling. Nevertheless, the truth of the matter is children leave home all the time before parents think it is the right time to do so. The parable of the Prodigal Son is a grand example. The son does not leave home because there are problems at home; the son leaves because he is looking for an adventure. The son leaves home merely because that is what he chooses to do. That is life.

It is instructive that in the story of the Prodigal Son the father does not chase after his child or attempt to restrain his wayward son. The father lets him go. Sometimes the greatest act of love is letting go. Nor does the father try to hide his hurt and disappointment. The father's family ball has fallen into the rough place of youth rebellion.

Like the wise man he is, the father chooses to play his ball where it lies. He suffers the loss of his son with dignity while clinging to the hope that someday his son will return home. This is the mode of living that attends those who choose to play it where it lies. Surely, the father must have suffered greatly when he saw other fathers and sons together. He must have spent many a sleepless night longing for his younger son. No doubt, he must have suffered the murmured whispers and sudden shifted glances that haunt those who have become the talk of the town. Yet, in all these sufferings and humiliation, the father remains steadfast and refuses to resort to subterfuge and fudgery.

For the father of the Prodigal Son, his hope is soon realized when his son comes to himself and returns home. So it could have been for the uncle. For did not his niece also return home? What then turned out to be a tragic tale could have been one of joy had the uncle only played it where it lies. As the judge who reported on this tragic case said, one "should never seek to excuse himself by false and undue means less thereby he, offending God (the author of truth), overthrow himself as the uncle did."[16]

Another benchmark of fudgers is that they have the same problem my students experience in my Introduction to Religious Studies course—they cannot tell the difference between a symbol and a sign. I tell them that a short-handed way of understanding that difference is that a symbol has to be interpreted whereas a sign does not. For instant, in the movie, "Duets," Huey Lewis wakes up one morning in bed with a woman he met at a bar the previous night. Draped around his neck is a cross. One cannot draw any conclusions from the meaning of that symbol as clearly it cannot mean to Lewis' character what it means to Christians who wear it. However, a sign that has "No Parking" printed on it does not need to be interpreted, although fudgers tend to do so. They ask such questions as, "Does it mean no parking unless I'm in a hurry?" "Does it mean no parking unless I can park, run my errand, and get back and leave before the parking enforcement officer arrives?" The treasuries of many towns and cities are kept overflowing by those who read signs as symbols.

I mention the uncle and the parking violator within the same few paragraphs to establish the point that there are no degrees of fudgery. A person is either a fudger or he/she is not. If a person parks in a spot where a sign says no parking, such a person is as much of a fudger as is the uncle. Most disaster movies begin with an act of fudgery. "Kingdom of the Spiders" begins with the overuse and improper use of pesticides. The "Alligator" series begins with the flushing of a baby alligator down the toilet. What appears in the beginning to be an innocuous act ends up having disastrous implications and brings about considerable evils for humankind. A split second decision or indecision can result in a lifetime of woe. A further example is in order.

Rule Number 7

Don't Trade Shame for Disaster

During the golden age of television, there was a marvelous program that aired regularly named "Death Valley Days," that at times was hosted by former President Ronald Reagan (before he had become president). One episode involved a young family who decided to move from the Midwest to California, where they hoped to take advantage of the opportunities offered by this western paradise. Upon arriving there, they discovered that the advertisements they had read were less than forthcoming, and California was not the paradise they had envisioned. Soon their meager funds are depleted and neither of them can find a job.

In an act of desperation, the husband/father attempts to rob a bank. He is caught and thrown in jail. The wife then tries to resort to that oldest of professions to raise the funds needed to get her husband out of jail on bond. Her first date is an undercover police officer, and she too is arrested. Now, both parents are in jail and their children are soon placed in foster care. The episode ends with this sad state of affairs. What started out as a dream has turned into a nightmare. That is the accustomed path of those who do not play it where it lies.

It is important to notice that there were several points at which this tragedy could have been avoided. One point, and perhaps the most critical one, was before this forlorn family made the journey. They left their jobs and went looking for work. It is a foolish thing indeed to leave a job and go looking for another one. One should always have another job before one quits the job one has. Perhaps it would have been better for one of them to go to California and locate a job and a place to live before the rest of the family packed up and moved there. I do not wish to rain on the idealism of this young couple or to make their dream of a better life into something profane. However, the best idealism is one tempered by realism. Our dreams always stand a better chance of being realized when we have a concrete plan that makes provisions for contingencies. The greatest platform on which to construct hope is wise planning.

Another point at which the tragedy could have been prevented was at the moment when their money got low and they could not find work. Perhaps that was the time to admit that they had erred and probably ought to return home or seek the assistance of family and friends back home, either to keep them going another few months in California, or to help them return home. One should always have family and friends to whom one can turn in a time of crisis. This is one of the reasons why I am not very sympathetic to homeless people, although I do support missions and programs designed to service them. I believe that being homeless says more about the homeless person than it does about society. What kind of person is it whose family and friends have shut him/her out in the cold?

Did not Robert Frost say in "The Hired Hand" that "home is a place you can always go back to and they have to take you in?" Of course, he said that before Thomas Wolfe, writing in the age of cynicism, said that "you can never go home again." I choose to cling to the wisdom of Frost that a person should be able to go home again.

I have not had to return home, except for visits, since I became an adult and left. Yet, it is refreshing and reassuring to know that if I needed to, I could go home and live with my mom. And not only with my mom, I have a number of siblings and friends with whom I could live were I caught in dire circumstances. That is how I have chosen to live my life and that is how people who play it where it lies live theirs. If, then, a person is truly homeless, should we help someone whose own families and friends have shut her or him out? Are we not enabling people to be irresponsible? Worst, are we not enabling persons to be fudgers? But I digress.

Returning to our young family, they found themselves with an unplayable lie. This was no time to fix the blame or to argue about who was responsible for them being in this predicament. During my short tenure as an assistant manager at Jack-in-the-Box, we had a motto that said, "Fix the breakdown not the blame." This was excellent advice for our forlorn couple. Unfortunately, they did not heed it. The husband blamed himself. With blame comes guilt. And with guilt comes a desperation that clouds the mind and inflames the passions and ends in disaster. So it was for his family. The disaster that befell them could have been avoided had they played it where it lies.

I can sympathize with this couple because I was in a similar situation in which I did not play it where it lies, and I suffered a near disaster. It occurred during the winter of 1973. Some of you will recall that was the year of the fuel crisis occasioned by O.P.E.C. I had gone to Detroit, Michigan, by automobile to spend Christmas with my daughter. On Christmas Eve, my daughter's mother and I got into an argument and I packed my bags and left.

I was so angry I neglected to ensure that I had sufficient fuel in the car. I was a number of miles outside of Detroit when I noticed I was nearly out of gas. There was not an open service station in sight. I continued on until the gas monitor was strangling "E". Then, I pulled into a closed service station, and there I remained until the day after Christmas. I almost froze to death. I ran my heater intermittently, hoping to preserve the few fumes remaining in the tank. But they, like the hope of our young couple, soon evaporated.

Anger got the best of me as it clouded my mind. Disaster was but a few degrees away. This incident happened before Juan taught me to play it where it lies. Now, no matter what the nature of the argument, on a cold winter's night and far from home, I will play it where it lies. I will heed the advice of B.B. King and leave, "As soon as the weather breaks!"

The episode of our young family ends without any resolve in sight. So far as I know, there were no sequels or further episodes in which this family was redeemed. Their ship of hope floundered on the shores of despair, and there they remained shipwrecked. This work is being written that you might be spared a similar fate. Tragedy need not be the final punctuation to our lives. We need not be shipwrecked if we can be rescued.

Rule Number 8

Beware of the Danger Ahead

I seek to rescue you, even as I have been rescued, before your ship crashes into the iceberg of absurdity or run aground on the shores of despair. I offer you the light of this path that you might avoid the dangers ahead by sailing around them. Be not like those who refused to believe that danger lay ahead because it could not be recorded on their instruments. There is more to existence than our technologies can perceive. As William James reminds us—there are different levels of consciousness—of reality. Our five senses and our instruments might miss many of those other levels of which James writes.

Take, for instance, a brief example from my own life. During one of my frequent journeys, I stopped at a local restaurant in Houston. When the waitress came to our table, for no apparent reason, I said to her, "I am so sorry to hear about what happened to you."

"How did you know? I haven't told a soul here. I just got into town last week and started working here today," she said as she sat down next to me and began to relate to me a most horrific story of how she had been kidnapped and held hostage by a former boyfriend who had been shot and killed by a police sharpshooter during the ordeal.

How could I have known what had happened to this woman whom I had never met and have neither spoken to nor seen since? Yet, someway and somehow there was a level of consciousness beneath our own conscious minds at which we had communicated. Perhaps my brain had sensed her pain—the same part of my brain that alerts me to my own pain had been stimulated by the pain of this young woman who had experienced a most traumatic event. Science may someday provide an explanation to what must for now remain a mystery.

Permit me one more short remembrance. During a previous journey to the Philippines, I met a young lady who was despondent because she had to leave college because her parents could no longer afford to pay her tuition and other school expenses. I agreed to provide her a scholarship so she could return to college. She thanked me and asked me if there was anything she could do for me.

"Yes, you can name your first child after me," I answered in a jovial tone of voice.

To my surprise, upon my next trip to the Philippines, I was asked to meet with her and her family. She was pregnant and had been pregnant during our earlier conversation. How could I have known that fact? Or, was this just a lucky guess or a matter of coincidence?

No doubt, this young lady and I had communicated on a deep unconscious level. Whether that communication was by spirit or one of the levels of consciousness suggested by William James, I cannot say. This is not to suggest that spirit itself is not a level of consciousness. In fact, what we call spirit may be nothing more than another level of consciousness—another way of perceiving different levels of reality.

We need not resolve this matter here. Our point is a simple one: that you cannot see an iceberg in the waters ahead nor record one on your navigational instruments should not convince you that the path ahead is clear. That your journey has been smooth sailing thus far is no guarantee that it will continue to be so. That you have "paid your dues" is no bar to your having to pay additional ones. Hence, the wisdom of reflecting on the light I offer you in this work. There may be danger ahead. That danger is real and may be present even though you may not be able to sense it. I can. I have.

Like the young waitress and the young student, I sense trouble in your life. Your ship is heading toward an iceberg. It has been thus ever since you fudged your ball along and got off course by a few degrees. In life, a few degrees expand with the passage of time until we are so far off course we find ourselves on the shores of North America instead of our intended India. And despite a momentary flair of success, we are soon cast into the dungeons of time, where the cold of darkness claims us, and we become fodder for the historical appetites of others.

I want to spare you such a fate. Thus it is that I am setting down on paper these words that, like the lighthouse of old, will shine light on the iceberg or rocks in your path that you might sail around them. Again, you are off course. You have been off course ever since you fudged your ball along the way when you thought that no one was looking. Some one was looking. I too saw you. Now, I offer you something denied the uncle and the young couple—redemption. However, this is the type of redemption which you must effectuate for yourself. There is not another who can do it for you. Others have made it possible for you to have another chance. Still, it is a chance that you must take. Like the game of jacks played by little girls in childhood, you have a chance to call "overs," and cast your jacks into a more favorable spread. Will you squander this chance as you did the first?

You are not persuaded. When did I see you? That is the question that lingers in your mind. Abandon it. It matters not when or how I saw you. What matters is that I did. I see you now. I see also all the things you have done when you thought the lights were out and no one was looking. You forgot that your soul is the Book of Life on which your thoughts, words, and deeds are recorded. It is as if you have a video camera embedded within you. This recording continues all the days of your life and records even while you are asleep. That is why it does not matter when and how I saw you. I can read it all anew now as I look into your eyes. There is no need for you to deny it—your ship is off course. Your life is a wreck.

By heeding these words, you can find the safe harbor. Don't worry that your ship may be traveling too fast to steer it safely. Your ship will turn in time and with ease the moment you get back on course ... by playing it where it lies.

3

THE RECKLESS

W hen I decided to hit my ball despite the fact that it was lodged against a tree, I went from being a fudger to being a reckless person. Juan advised me that it was error to attempt to hit the ball where it lay. Not only would hitting at the ball pose an unnecessary risk of damage to the club or iron I used, it could cause injury to me and could damage the tree. I ignored this advice and proceeded on. In doing so, I took an unnecessary risk. Not only was the risk unnecessary, my taking it was foolish and reckless. As a result, my position in the game of golf was exacerbated. The recklessness of my actions was driven home to me during my recent trip to the Philippines.

Rule Number 9
Don't Chase Chickens!

There, I visited a family, the wife of which had invited me to her home to speak with her abusive husband. While sitting on the porch watching the husband assist his wife in picking through a bushel of beans, I noted that several of their chickens had intruded upon the rice they had spread out on a bamboo cover on the ground. "Why don't you stop them?" I asked.

"Why? They'll just keep comin back and I will wear myself out. Let 'em alone and they will get fed and maybe even clean out a few worms."

I was amazed at the simple wisdom of this man. Clearly, he was not the ogre I had envisioned. Yet, there was a problem to be solved. Seizing upon his lesson in futility, we discussed chickens, rice, and beans. I mostly listened and asked questions, and occasionally related our conversation to life and to people. Not once did I mention his relationship with his wife or the matter she had shared with me. I did, however, compliment him on being a wonderful provider for his family and how much they must adore and love him. I also mentioned how much he must love and respect his wife, to be sitting on the front porch picking beans, unafraid that one of his male friends might walk by and think him to be less than a man.

When I stood up to leave, his wife asked me to pray. I prayed a prayer of thanksgiving in which I thanked God for this man who is such a blessing to his family, and for the love and fellowship which the entire family shared. I was overjoyed to receive a letter from his local pastor recently that this man, who has never attended church with his wife, has opened up a Bible study within his home. More importantly, the pastor reports that he is no longer abusing his wife. Here is an example of a man who was enlightened by philosophy, and this opened him up to seek a spiritual path as well. Of course, only time will tell whether his attendance at Bible Study is solely to placate his wife, or whether his interest is genuine and an indication for further growth.

Like the man and his chickens, we face similar situations in the game of life in which we find ourselves engaged in futile or reckless activity. Unlike the man, we do not come to a quick and early realization of the futility of our actions. A simple example will suffice. How many times have we been late for an appointment, and, as a result, we exceeded the speed limit? Sometimes, we get stopped by a police officer and the resulting ticket and lecture further delay us, and now we are even later and have added to our burdens because we have a ticket to deal with. Then there are times when our speeding results in our being in an accident, and we are not only delayed, we may not make our appointment at all. However, had we gone the speed limit, the penalty to be paid for being late would not have been nearly as severe as the one we paid for speeding and being late. Life is a given but life is not free. We have to pay the costs associated with the game of life, and this means that we have to assess our risks and not take unnecessary ones or engage in futile activities. We must live life with authenticity and intentionality. Like the Gambler, we too have to know when to "hold em" and when to "fold em."

We must live our lives as if our lives were a vehicle. Notice that a vehicle has a reverse and several forward gears. That is because no matter how good a driver we are, sometimes we have to back up. The same is true in life. Moving forward is the preferred direction of our travel. However, sometimes, to move forward we have to first move backward. We may discover an obstacle in the road ahead that does not appear on our map, or we may find that the road is worse than we anticipated. There could even be a wreck or some other factor which causes us to back up. We must be willing to back up without interpreting such a move as a retreat. We do not wish to play semantics here, so, if one insists on labeling our move a retreat, we can say, as General Houston must have said during the Texas Revolution, that our retreat is one into victory.

Rule Number 10

Playing It Where It Lies Requires Making Choices

Part of the cost of living is making choices. Our degree of success in the game of life depends, in part, on how well we make these choices, and how sound our decisions are. Our success is also contingent upon our not only listening to the advice of our coach but following it unless we are confident that our contrary position is the right one for us at the time. Notice, I said "confident" and not "sure" because ultimately, we can never be sure of our decisions. That is part of the risk we take when we play the game of life.

Speaking of not being sure, when I say that I had hit my ball into an unplayable lie, that is not completely accurate. At least, it is not completely accurate from a philosophical perspective. That is because what golf calls an "unplayable lie" is a misnomer. The lie can be played—it is just a matter of how one chooses to play it. Even if one takes the penalty stroke and drops the ball to a new location or walks back to the tee and hits the ball from that location, one is playing what golf has called an unplayable lie. The same is true in the game of life. What oftentimes appears as an unplayable lie is but an opportunity to be creative. It is said that the Chinese word for crisis also means opportunity. That is a wise saying indeed, as the following will demonstrate.

For instance, it can be argued that the circumstances of my birth gave me an unplayable lie. No doubt, many with less chances than I have been afforded and who did not have the kind of positive people who have come in and out of my life, might have abandoned the game long ago or entered upon a course of reckless conduct. I was born the fifth of what would be a family of 22 children in Fort Worth, Texas. Our family was poor but happy. Were it not for government commodities, we might have starved to death on many occasions.

My mother was first a domestic worker, then a pastry cook until the civil rights era opened up more job opportunities for African-Americans, at which time she went to work for a local electronics firm. My father initially was a cook, then a construction worker, and lastly he worked at one of the local meat packing plants. He was the consummate hard worker. After working all day or all night, he would come home and junk cars—he would buy old wrecked cars, then cut them up and sell the parts, and the rest he would sell for scrap metal.

For most of my youth, the only Christmas we received was that provided by charitable organizations, to which I am eternally grateful. Despite this lie, my parents instilled within us the value of hard work and honesty. Our father was wont to remind us quite frequently that he had never stolen anything or been inside a jail house. He was quite proud of those two factors. My mom would often say he was just damn lucky that he had not been arrested for drunkenness. Our father did enjoy a good Pearl or Jax beer and an unfiltered Camel cigarette.

Early on, we were taught the need for an abiding faith and church attendance. These became critical to us, although each of us have struggled with exactly what they mean and the extent of their hold on our lives. As we got older, we tended to make church attendance less a part of our regular activities, at least which has been the case for all but four or five of us, though, I am happy to say, that number is ever increasing. Despite the fact that I was an "A" student throughout secondary school, I dropped out of high school in the eleventh grade because I was bored. I looked around and saw the youth rebellion and the civil rights movement literally blazing trails in our cities, and I wanted to be part of those movements. So I dropped out of high school and became a drunk. That move increased the unplayable nature of my lie. Thankfully, that is not the end of the story.

An enterprising truant officer advised me of the benefits of going into the job corps, and I went there and earned my general equivalency diploma. I could have continued in my state of resignation. However, even though I had not yet been indoctrinated to the way of life unveiled in this book, its scent had invaded my nostrils, and I began to sense that I could get back into the game. And so I did.

After a brief stint in the Army, I enrolled in college, and it seems as if I have been in school ever since.

One of the points I wish to make in relating this biographical data is that the way of life being offered here I have traveled myself and though I have not yet achieved the victory, the checkered flag is in view. Another point is this, no matter where you, the reader, are in your own life, you too can get back in the game and start moving toward your own victory lap. The key is to stay in the game. And if you have checked out of it, get back in before it is too late. Do not "go gently into that good night" but rage against the mediocre life and the intentional and the unintentional death by suicide. Do not give up your chance to play this marvelous game of life and move toward that heavenly banquet for the mere crumbs that fall from the table of the world. If I can do it, so can you. Do not think yourself to be making a sacrifice when, in fact, you are making surren-der—another hallmark of reckless conduct.

In her epochal work, *The Virtue of Selfishness*, a work which continues to influence me and which rescued me early on from mediocrity, Ayn Rand writes of the dichotomy between sacrifice and surrender. Sacrifice is to give up something great for something greater, whereas surrender is to give up something great for some-thing of lesser value. In every reckless act, we surrender something great for something of lesser value. We should never want something so bad that we are willing to do anything to get it or to keep it. We should always assess the risks associated with our actions and back away when the risks outweigh the benefits. Consequently, even if I succeeded in moving my ball, it would not compensate for the risk I was taking and the ball would not be in a better lie than if I accepted the penalty outright and moved the ball according to the rules of golf. A further example comes to mind.

Rule Number 11
Never Risk A Lot To Gain A Little

When I was practicing law in Texas, I had occasion to represent a young man who was charged with the attempted theft of a Christmas tree. The tree was valued at a little over $40. To get out of jail, the young man had to post bail of $500 which cost him $120. My fee was $500. He received un-adjudicated probation for six months which cost him $375, including court costs. Thus, the young man took a risk in which he ended up paying over $1,000 for a tree that he did not get to keep. Moreover, he risked much more for the tree than the tree was worth, for he could have been sentenced up to six months in jail and fined up to five-hundred dollars. Clearly, the young man surrendered a great thing for something of lesser value. He was reckless. He refused to play it where it lies.

No doubt, the young man's ball had lodged against a tree. He had failed to plan for Christmas, and he found himself near the holiday without a tree for his family. He was broke, it was Christmas time, and he had a family depending on him. This was a less than favorable lie. Nevertheless, there were other responses to the young man's dilemma. For instance, he could have tried to borrow the money. He could have tried working for the tree. Or, he could have paid the penalty for not planning for Christmas and suffered the pain of telling his family they would not have a tree that year, but he would make it up to them the following year. There were additional responses as well, such as contacting some social or charitable agency for assistance. Many churches and religious organizations provide varying degrees of assistance during the holiday season. As I stated above, there were many Christmases that my family would have had nothing were it not for charitable organizations. We were not too proud to ask for and to receive help.

The young man is not alone. (Actually, he was not alone the night of the crime—he had two buddies with him who were also arrested and paid costs very similar to what he had to pay.) Countless people every day engage in conduct that risks more than they stand to gain. Take the young people who drag race through neighborhood streets. One would think they would have gotten the message of the classic movie, *Rebel Without A Cause.* Yet, these young people continue to engage in a meaningless event from which all they can hope to gain is a momentary psychological high and the worthless admiration of fools like themselves. All the while they are risking the most precious gift we humans can ever be given—the gift of life.

Another example is found in that marvelous movie, *I Want To Live*, starring Susan Hayward. The character played by Hayward longs to live yet acts in such a way as to lose the very thing she desires to preserve. She wants to live. However, she lives in such a way as to bring about her imminent death.

Unnecessary risk is not the only hallmark of the reckless. The other indication is doing something that is futile. Therapists know this very well and oftentimes ask their patients to recite the definition of insanity. When the patient cannot do so, the therapist then says that "Insanity is doing the same thing over and over again expecting different results." Insanity is doing something that is futile. It is like Thelma and Louise going over the cliff in their convertible as if they could escape this field of play and land in another one. Surely, they did escape as so many suicides do every day. However, it is futile to think one can solve a problem that way or secure another lie. All they found at the bottom of the cliff over which they drove their car was that cold and final darkness into which so many go and from which none return. As Dylan Thomas advised, "Don't go gently into that good night ..."

Beating one's head against the proverbial wall is also futile. A prevalent example occurs in relationships. I have recently concluded counseling a young married couple who, despite only three years of marriage, have already grown distant from one another. They no longer do anything together, and the husband is always drunk. The husband had sworn off drinking when the future wife had consented to marry him. He "fell off the wagon" mid-way through the first year of marriage. They have a two-year-old son. They are both gainfully employed, and the wife is attending classes at the local community college.

The husband attended only one counseling session. The wife attended three sessions, two without her husband. I refused to schedule more sessions unless the husband showed up. I asked him on the telephone if he wanted a divorce. He responded no. And yet, he refused to take any action to save his marriage. He refused to attend counseling with me or anyone else, and he refused to stop drinking. His ball is lodged against a tree, and he keeps swinging away without moving the ball. All the while, he is incurring penalty strokes. His actions are futile. He is reckless. And when the wife tires of this futile existence and seeks a divorce, he will become bitter and enraged and will curse the unfairness of life and "the system." He probably will never come to see the futility of his action/non-action. He is squandering a marvelous opportunity to carve out of the pie of life a slice of happiness.

Similarly, I have a friend who drinks too much. His father killed himself in a car wreck in which the son was seriously injured. I represented my friend in a driving while intoxicated case that happened a few years after the death of his father. I asked him why did he continue to drink, especially given his father's death and his near death—both as a result of drinking. He offered no reasons. I tried to explain to him that his body was already programmed to drunkenness by his father, and that he could overcome that only by not drinking. He should not drink at all because of the propensity of his body toward alcoholism. He did not heed my advice. He subsequently lost his job and his family. He is now living with relatives and friends. Soon he will join the ranks of the homeless if he does not kill himself first. He still drinks. He refuses to play it where it lies. He is living a futile existence. He too is reckless.

With each drink this young man is condemning himself to a mediocre existence. The more he drinks, the less chance he has of breaking the chains that currently bind him and that keep him from moving forward. He is closing doors of opportunity while complaining that the system is against him. He is making himself unemployable while daily cursing the system that refuses to employ him. Like Camus' guest, he is walking down the road of destruction with eyes wide open.

Contrary to these two examples of futility, I have another friend, named Charles Smith, with whom I became friends while representing him for involuntary manslaughter. One night while drunk, he plowed his vehicle into the back of another vehicle that had stopped in the road ahead. A 13 year-old little girl was killed in the ensuing crash. This was the seventh time Charles had been arrested for driving while intoxicated. And yet, he had continued to drink and drive. Now, he had killed a young girl.

I counseled with Charles about the mess he had gotten into, and that the only possible way I could help him would be if he first helped himself. Charles heeded my advice, and, for the first time in his life he sought serious help for his drinking problem. I was able to get Charles a probated sentence for five years. I am proud to report that he is now 10 plus years into sobriety and is the owner of a heating and air conditioning business in the Fort Worth/Dallas, Texas, area. Charles went from being reckless to playing it where it lies. He had to admit to himself that there are many people who can drink. He is not one of them. It is tragic that a little girl had to die for him to learn this lesson. Yet, so many others go on and on, without ever playing it where it lies and the body count keep rising.

It is critical that we note that the change wrought in Charles was not the result of religion or theology. Charles was not traveling along the road to Emmaus when a stranger joined him and convinced him that he was walking with the Christ, and as a result he came to realize that he needed to change his life. Nor was he suddenly struck down on the road to Damascus and blinded by a light that called him to greater service. Charles accepted the critique that he was not playing it where it lies, and, if he was to avoid prison and certain destruction, he needed to make a change in his life and outlook.

Rule Number 12

Do Not Risk Killing Yourself for Pleasure

Part of what it means to play it where it lies is to recognize our own weaknesses and proclivities. Like buildings, our bodies may be constructed in such a way that makes certain activities unsuitable. It may be that the abuses of drugs and/or alcohol by our forbears have damaged our bodies to such an extent that just a little drugs or alcohol will push us over the edge. If so, this is our lie. We have to play it by refusing to engage in drugs and alcohol. We may even have to distance ourselves from any activities involving these things. That is part of what it means to live an authentic existence. We have no control over the circumstances, of our birth; however, we can go beyond those circumstances as I have demonstrated by sharing with you a snapshot from my own life. We can say "woe is me," and stand there hacking away at our ball. Or, we can pick it up, accept our penalty stroke, and move forward with the game of life.

It is foolish to engage in an activity that we know will cause us harm for the mere pleasure of engaging in the activity. I am not speaking here of the many heroes who risk their lives every day to save persons and property—like the brave young men and women who rushed inside the World Trade Center buildings and perished in the resulting collapse of that icon of Western economics. The activities of which I speak have no redeeming qualities. Perhaps the best example is that of smoking. How humans ever seized upon such a vile and rancid activity is beyond my comprehension. I can think of no human activity more offensive to common sense and more bereft of reason than smoking. Smoking is the absurdity of absurdities.

Nevertheless, countless numbers of people engage in the reckless conduct of smoking. People smoke just as they participate in other activities that put at risk their lives for little or nothing in return. Such people are surrendering the precious gift of life. They squander an opportunity for both a qualitative and quantitative life and all they get in return is shortness of breath and shortness of life. Like the young people of whom we spoke earlier who speed themselves to death when there is so much living to be done. This is the essence of the reckless—surrendering to less than what life holds out for them. It is much like the prince who gives up his royal clothes to live the life of a pauper just for the thrill of seeing what it is like to live in the gutter. Living in the gutter, he forfeits the opportunity to lift people out of it.

Consider the number of people who have splashed their lives over the rocks of Niagara Falls. They have thrown away a marvelous gift in return for a cold, watery grave. This is a reckless act. For even if they had succeeded, what would have been their reward? Fifteen minutes of fame, then a quick return to obscurity or confinement in some institution, where the misery of their life will be increased. Does anyone remember the name of the last person to survive going over the Falls? Isn't life worth much more than that?

This book answers with a resounding yes. Life is always worth living, and it is too precious a gift to squander for 15 minutes of fame. No matter what lie we find ourselves in, as the abusive husband and Charles demonstrate, we can remain in the game and achieve some level of success. Even if we must incur a penalty stroke, we can accept it and move on. A mistake need not be fatal. A shift in the winds of time need not condemn us nor circumscribe our position in life. Following the yellow-brick road did not shield little Dorothy and her companions from evil and misfortune. However, it nevertheless led them to their goal and the realization of their dreams. Likewise will this path, though it will not make you impervious to the slings and arrows of misfortune, it will ensure that you will arrive at your destination. Your greatest challenge is to stay on it.

Ignore the call of the Sirens that would bid you to detour to the shores of discontent and the island of self indulgence. Though their song is enchanting, resist it and stay focused on the way ahead. To leave this path is to be reckless. To seek another way is futile.

4

THE PROS

The rules of golf envision that there will be times when golfers will hit into an unplayable lie. There are at least three rules for addressing this situation as explained by Russell:

Player A discovers his tee ball in an area of trees, at the corner of a dogleg right hole—a hole that winds to the right. He knows that the ball is unplayable. Yet, taking the option to drop the ball within two club lengths of the spot where it lies and no nearer the hole, under penalty of one stroke, will not help him. That's because, after dropping the ball, it would still be so close to the trees that he would not be able to send it flying up quickly enough to avoid them. He also doesn't want to incur a one-stroke penalty, walk back to the tee, 210 yards away, and hit his third shot. He chooses the third available option, according to Rule 28 of *The Rules of Golf*: to walk back as far as he wants, keeping the point where the original ball lay between the hole and where he drops the ball (87).

Rule Number 13

Avoid Living in the Default Margins of Life

We have seen in preceding chapters how the fudger and the reckless person would proceed. It may be that they are not fully aware of their options. That is no excuse. For we have also discussed how ignorance of the law is no excuse for the commission of a crime. If one is going to play a game, one ought to take the time to learn the rules of the game and to attain the requisite skills. It is amazing how many parents have never read a book on parenting. Imagine the problems they could have avoided, the mistakes they would not have made, had they taken the time to read at least one such book. No doubt, there will be many returns and telephone calls to 800 numbers the day after Christmas because so many people will unwrap items and attempt to assemble and to use them, without ever taking the time to read the instruction manual. For far too many people, reading the instructions is usually a last resort.

Recently, I sent a text message to a friend of mine. A few days later I saw her and asked her why she had not responded. She said that she did not know she had text messaging and did not know how to send one. She was using her cell phone in the default mode. Of course, she had no explanation why she did not telephone me since she could not use text messaging.

Think of all the troubled relationships that are floundering on the rocks of despair because those involved refuse to seek outside help or to attend a weekend retreat, counseling session or sit down together and read a book or two on relationships. Like the young couple we met earlier, their "moonlight kisses" are fading in "the warmth of the sun" because they refuse to seek the help they need to salvage their relationship. Oh, what needless losses.

Sometimes it is pride that gets in the way. At other times, it is simply ignorance. Still, and probably most often, it is that one or more of these people have reached an unplayable lie, and rather than explore their options and do what is necessary to move forward, they either stand whacking away at the ball that is either not moving very far or getting more deeply ingrained in the brush, or they pick up their clubs and abandon the game altogether. Such persons are less than amateurs and hence the greatness of their failures.

For example, consider the tragic tale of Chante Mallard, a 27-year-old nurse's aid living and working in Fort Worth, Texas.[17] One night, invigorated with the date drug Ecstasy and oiled by alcohol, this young lady spends a long night partying with her friends at a local nightspot. On her way home during those bewitching hours following midnight, her automobile struck a homeless man who was catapulted into her windshield. Undaunted by this unfortunate turn of events, Chante continued her drive home with the man embedded in her windshield.

Upon arriving at home, she pulled into her garage and left the man there. Several times throughout the night, she returned to the man and whispered to him how sorry she was. Meanwhile, she telephoned her boyfriend who came over and comforted her with more alcohol and marijuana while they engaged in passionate sex.

The unfortunate homeless man, later identified as 37-year-old Gregory Biggs, gave up the ghost and passed into that eternal darkness.

The next day, Chante and her boyfriend noticed that Biggs was dead, so they telephoned some friends who came over and helped them to dispose of the body. Only the random act of someone close to her who made an anonymous call to the police department brought to light this horrible tale, which for four months had been relegated to the closet of family secrets.

Chante was eventually arrested and brought to trial. Despite a forceful and valiant defense, she was found guilty of murder and sentenced to 50 years in prison. How did this happen? How could this young lady, trained and skilled in the science of preserving life and comforting the afflicted, stray so far from the path to which she had been assigned? Was it the drugs, the alcohol, the bewitching hour? Surely, Florence Nightingale must have turned over in the proverbial grave at the sight of this tragedy.

It is instructive to note that this was not a case of a lack of having the proper tools or a failure to instruct, nor can it be attributed to inexperience. This young lady had been properly trained and had worked many years as a nurse's aid. Several of her former clients testified at her trial on her behalf. And yet, this player in the game of life faced an unplayable lie. And what did she do? She took out her iron and started whacking away at the ball which moved only deeper into the brush. With each whack, she dug herself deeper into trouble and locked the door more securely on her future jail cell.

What was it that kept this young woman from perceiving more clearly her predicament and moving her with compassion toward the man she had injured? Where in her life had she learned the ethical stance that saying she is sorry makes everything all right? We will have to wait many years for answers to these and other questions until she has been observed, tested, and evaluated by competent professionals.

All we can conclude at this juncture is that she faced an unplayable lie and refused to play it where it lies. Like our forlorn couple, she faced many opportunities to salvage her life and career, but she slaughtered them all. Even the next morning, after cool reflection, she could have possibly escaped a charge of murder and faced a charge of involuntary manslaughter. However, the light of day could not bring her out of the darkness to which she had consigned herself. The heat of the morning sun could not defrost the ice that had formed around her heart. Are you, dear reader, any better?

Rule Number 14
Shortcuts Often Lead to Longsuffering

Unlike the persons described above, the pro is one who not only has read the rules but knows them, and has developed the requisite skills to play the game, and continues to practice. Continuing to develop and sharpen his/her skills, the pro learns to avoid an unplayable lie and to play it when it presents itself. For one of the things that the pro must learn is how to assess risk. This is because being a pro does not mean avoiding an unplayable lie. Sometimes, facing the unplayable lie elevates us to the status of pro, like the triumph of Charles over his alcoholism. What makes a pro is oftentimes decided by the choices made in the face of difficulty and trial. Each of the options the pro faces when playing an unplayable lie involves some risk.

The pro has to be willing to assess that risk, face it, and choose the risk that presents the best advantage under all the circumstances. It is this assessment of risk that separates the pro from the reckless person. Some risks are just not worth taking while others fall within acceptable limits. Another difference between the pro and the fudger or reckless person is that the pro is willing to accept the penalty for his/her mistake even as s/he struggles to avoid the penalty.

While we do not know the reasons why the uncle's niece chose to run away from home, we do know that he was not willing to pay the penalty for her having done so. He chose instead to weave a web of deceit that in the end cost him a greater penalty than the one he faced initially. The young man who attempted to steal the Christmas tree entered upon a course of action that resulted in his having to pay a much greater penalty than he faced initially. A pro would not be caught in such situations. For the pro knows and accepts the fact that penalties are part of the game. Ever notice how basketball players raise their hands when the whistle blows signaling they have committed a foul? The basketball player says "I did it and I am willing to pay the penalty assessed." This does not stop some players from protesting their fouls at times; however, as a general rule the player raises his hand and goes on. That is the mark of a pro.

When I was a teenager, my mother had a Chevrolet Nova that I truly enjoyed driving. One day I was driving in downtown Dallas and pulled into a parking lot that required a two-dollar parking fee upon exiting. I ran my errand and when I returned

I drove over the curb to avoid paying the fee. In doing so, I damaged one of the tire rods on the car. The cost to repair it? Seventy dollars! Many readers of this book will be able to search their own lives and discover times when they too tried to save a buck or two only to pay more in the end. Shortcuts often lead to long suffering.

Sometimes in life, penalties have to be paid. It is akin to driving. No matter how good a driver we are, sooner or later we are going to have to put our automobile in reverse and back up—sometimes, we will have to turn completely around. This lesson is dramatized in that wonderful novel by Lorenz Graham entitled, "South Town." At the end of the novel, the Williams family discovers that they must abandon their home and move north if David, the son, is to realize his dream of becoming a doctor, and the father is to secure a decent job at a decent wage. In giving their assent to this change, they have to give up their farm, their friends, and the life that has been theirs for so long. They have to give up their independence and face the possibility of having to live with relatives for a while. However, these wise people know that if they are to have a chance at winning at the game of life, they must play it where it lies and pay the penalty for having an unplayable lie—even though their lie is the result of racism and injustice.

Rule Number 15

Sometimes We Have to Retreat Into Victory

Compare the Williams to our forlorn family whose dreams crashed against the rocks of absurdity in California. This latter family tried at every turn to avoid the penalty they faced for having played into an unplayable lie. Each time they attempted to escape, they found themselves deeper in the trap from which they were trying to emerge. So it is for those who try to avoid paying a penalty they have incurred, only to discover that they have to pay an even greater penalty for their failed attempt to avoid their "unplayable lie."

Or, reflect with me for a moment on that historical event during the Texas Revolution, when General Sam Houston was forced to "retreat into victory." What a terror must have seized the people of the Lone Star State, as news spread that their shining knight in armor was in retreat. Little did the people or Santa Anna, the general of the Mexican Army, know that this retreat was part of the plan of the general to gain time to recruit and train a mighty army. And so the general continued his retreat (thanks to additional time granted him by the heroes at the Alamo) all the way to San Jacinto, where he encountered and defeated Santa Anna, and added another star to the celestial crown of that wondrous galaxy we call the United States of America.

Both the Williams and General Houston played into an unplayable lie. Yet, each responded with dignity and grace, and both achieved a mighty victory. The hosts of heaven must have sung glorious songs of joy even as they wiped the tears away from eyes that had seen so many noble souls fall into that cold dark night that others might continue in the heat of day. Their lives were not in vain—nor were their roles of being fodder with which to fuel the fires of others. They too had played into an unplayable lie and they too responded with dignity and grace.

There are times when our ball goes into the rough due to no fault of our own. Sudden shifts in the wind, crowd noise, or some other factor might be the culprit. At other times, we can point with certainty to some action or inaction on our part that caused the unplayable lie. In either case, the measure of the level of our competency is reflected in our response. The same is true for us in the game of life.

It matters little how we got into an unplayable lie. Like workers at Jack-in-the-Box, we need to focus on fixing the breakdown and not the blame. Consequently, the measure of whom and what we are comes not in our ability to avoid an unplayable lie, for oftentimes these situations are part of the so-called "facts of life." Rather, the test of our character comes in how we respond to a given situation. We cannot always control what happens to us. We can and should control how we respond.

Imagine how different history would have been had former President Nixon gone before the American people and admitted that certain members of his staff had committed criminal acts on his watch, and that he accepted full responsibility for it and deeply regretted their errors. Perhaps he could have shed a few tears as he had done in his famous "Checkers Speech." No doubt, the result would have been the same—the American people would have forgiven him, and he would have completed his term in office.

Nixon faced an unplayable lie. His political ball was lodged against a tree. Rather than accept the penalty and move on, he chose to fudge his ball along, and, in the end, he lost the game. Somehow, he went from being a pro, as he had been during the Checkers Speech, to being a reckless and self-destructive person. He is not alone.

Former President Clinton could have avoided international disgrace had he been a pro about his affair with a young intern. He too played into an unplayable lie and rather than accept the penalty and move on, he took an unnecessary risk that almost derailed his presidency and his marriage. Had it not been for Kenneth Starr, who turned Clinton into an underdog (Americans almost always side with the underdog—especially a persecuted one.), Clinton would have followed Nixon into relative obscurity.

Rule Number 16

Being A Pro Makes A Difference in Life

For both Nixon and Clinton, their misconduct following the underlying crime was much worst than the crime itself. The penalties they paid far exceeded the ones they would have paid had they confessed to the crime, paid their penalty, and moved on. Neither leader was a pro. Contrast their conduct to that of Martha Stewart, who, regardless of whether she was guilty, she accepted her penalty and went to prison. It is instructive to note that she hired a corrections expert to advise her on the ways of incarceration. Stewart was wise enough to know that prison, like life, has rules, and if one is to succeed at the game, one needs to know the rules. Stewart became a pro, and no doubt she will recover from her failure and secure her place in the pantheon of heroes.

Earlier, we discussed Gershwin and how, when he was commissioned to write a piano concerto, he consulted others and read a book on the subject. Gershwin was the quintessential pro. He admitted he did not know how to write a piano concerto then secured the necessary skills.

Too many people experience difficulty saying three little words: "I don't know." Such people think it is a sign of weakness and intellectual deficiency to admit a lack of knowledge. They fudge the truth, give speculative answers, lie, and literally make fools of themselves as well as bring about disastrous consequences—all because they cannot admit they do not know the answer to the question posed to them.

A dramatic portrayal of this truth is represented in Flannery O'Connor's short story, "A Good Man Is Hard to Find." There, a mother refuses to admit that she does not know the way to the intended destination, and the son refuses to confront his mother or to disregard her directions. Consequently, the mother, her son, his wife and children all lose their lives—a tragedy which could have been avoided. All the mother had to do was to admit that she did not know the way. Neither the mother nor the son was a pro. Neither of them knew how to play it where it lies.

Another simpler illustration is in order. Recently, I sought to order a subway sandwich for the students of one of my classes. I went to a Subway in Victorville, California, and spent 15 minutes making the appropriate selections. As the young lady began to ring up my order, I asked her if it would be difficult for me to handle the sandwich after they sliced it.

"Oh, we don't slice them," she replied.

I almost responded in a flippant manner. However, I asked her politely whether she could make an exception. She responded in the negative. At that moment, I could have done as so many others. I could have questioned her as to the rationale of such a policy and expressed my anger and frustration that she had wasted my time. However, I realized that I faced an unplayable lie. This restaurant did not slice six-foot submarine sandwiches, and all the talk and anger in the world was not going to alter that fact. I could work myself into frenzy, but it would be to no avail. Realizing this state of affairs, I thanked the young lady and left. This is what it means to play it where it lies.

I had to travel to the next city, where I was able to secure what I wanted at a Blimpi's. There, not only did they slice the sandwich at no additional charge, they offered to help me carry it to my car. I exchanged stress for convenience and saved myself a great deal of psychological and physical discomfort. In doing so, though I did not know it at the time, I became a subject in my own philosophical trial. The result proves the viability of the path being revealed here and demonstrates that we can be pros in our everyday affairs.

It is not just in the grand confrontations in our lives that a sound and viable philosophy is required. We need such a path even in the mundane trenches of life. A little bump in the road can cause severe damage to a vehicle that moves too swiftly over it. A little spark can cause a devastating blaze.

The pro is able to recognize and to negotiate the obstacles in the road ahead. Moreover, the pro possesses the requisite tools and has undergone the necessary training to ensure the journey undertaken will be successful. It is unfortunate that the captain of the Titanic was not a pro. What tragedy befell his crew and passengers because he had not learned how to play it where it lies.

5

THE NOVICE

There was a point during that first golf game when I considered giving up the idea of playing golf. Actually, there were several such points. There were moments when I seriously thought about saying to hell with golf and walking off the course. I entertained quitting even before I had learned the rules of the game and developed the skill needed to play golf at a competitive level. I wanted to give up at the lowest level of the game—that of a novice.

The first point at which I wanted to bail out was when I had to buy shoes and rent clubs and irons. I wanted to play the game of golf but did not want to pay the costs of doing so. Golf is an expensive game. I can play several games of bowling for what my green fee cost. Then there is all the equipment one needs to play golf. In bowling, one can rent shoes and the ball is free. Not so in golf.

Rule Number 17
Life Costs

That is one of the reasons I have likened the game of life to the game of golf. Life costs. I have to think, to plan, to work, to make decisions and to accept responsibility for the choices I make. There are times when I have the best of intentions, and yet the worst of results attend my efforts. There are times when I have done all my homework and planned and thought and prayed, and still things go wrong. There are times my senses fail me, my reason deserts me, and my heart lets me down. And still, I have to bear the brunt of the misery resulting from these failures. Life costs. Did not the Buddha spend a lifetime warring against suffering only to die defeated by the agony of food poisoning?

I want to break free of the demands and restraints of living. I want a life that is free—that is without costs. I do not want to carry the burdens of making choices. Just once I would like to be able to live without worry of the outcome of what I do. What ecstasy I could achieve if I could lose myself in my wife's embrace and not have to guard against calling her the name of some former lover. Or compliment the dress or beauty of a female stranger without incurring her scorn and accusation that I am a sexist. How glorious life would be to embrace children without passersby casting stones at what they perceive is prurient and inappropriate behavior. I want to strip myself of the burden of clothes and run bare to the beach and dive into the ocean and swim toward the distant horizon.

And yet, I know that even then there would be costs. There is no escaping them. If I shed my clothes and head for the beach, I might not make it, for either the police or the men in the white robes will intercept me and carry me in a different direction. The rules of law and morals would not be suspended by my own wishes. And even if I made it to the ocean, the laws of nature would not dim to the blazing of my fires of rebellion. In the midst of the ocean there would be costs: sharks might find me an unexpected blessing of a meal; the undercurrent might pull me in a direction I do not intend to go; the horizon would become ever more distant the nearer I tried to reach it. I would never be able to touch the horizon. Soon, my body would tire of my rebellion and collapse into the ocean; thus would end my folly. And oh what a cost would I have to pay. My life! Life costs.

Today, the fires within me blaze, and I want to escape the costs of living. I stand in my small courtyard and look toward the heavens. It is a cool and windy day. Thick gray clouds blanket the sky. I want to mount wings like Icarus and sail beyond the clouds. Or even more so, like the Silversurfer of my youth, I want to surf the cosmic waves. There, too, am I defeated before I take the first step. For though I could rise above my earth-bound limitations, the laws of physics would come into play, and soon I would crash into that glass ceiling that has sent so many others, including Icarus, crashing to earth. Again, I would have to pay a heavy cost for my attempt to escape the costs of living.

So I turn to the mystics of ancient times and, in a desperate move, I lie prostrate, close my eyes and try to enter the cloud of unknowing.

Perhaps, I hope, if I cannot escape the heaviness of my body, I can release my spirit. I try all the incantations. I even seek the "stillness." Nothing is achieved but deep relaxation. I turn to the astral plane. Yet, even there I am denied. For how can I tell where my mind ends and my spirit begins? Did not the Apostle Paul stumble at the same point? Did he too not wonder whether he had traveled in the body or in the spirit?[18] How can I extend the silver cord if I cannot discern the boundaries of my mind and my spirit? How will I ever know if I have traveled outside the deep wells of my unconsciousness? Now, my head hurts! It costs even when we attempt to escape the costs of life.

Life costs. It is an immutable rule of the game of life. And like golf, if I want to play the game, I have to be willing to pay the costs of doing so. Monumental and sometimes ephemeral tragedies have resulted from human efforts to escape the costs of life. In a post-9/11 world, one of the costs we have to pay to go on living is to become increasingly conscious of our surroundings and security concerns. We have to become more aware of the lives of people around the world, and we have to be active in our efforts to improve the quality of life for all people everywhere—even people with whom we disagree. The costs of our way of life in the West have been increased dramatically as we have had to come to the realization that there is a reality to the saying of old: "To those to whom much is given, much is required."

Surely, many of us would like to be left alone to enjoy the fruits of our labor. "If people do not like our way of life, then let them create a better one," we tell ourselves. No sooner do the words escape our lips do we see them evaporate under the sun of absurdity that reminds us we can no longer live in isolation. When the World Trade Center buildings collapsed, so too did our walls of isolation. We must now pay the price for being a world power and having such a "superior" culture. We must pay the costs of being "one nation under God" which God has blessed and sustained with blessings beyond counting.

Like lovers who must now be aware of the criminals who lurk in the shadows of lovers lanes, we too must be aware of those who lurk in the shadows of discontent and meager lives. For in both cases, those who live in the shadows seek to destroy those of us who occupy the darkness for only a brief moment of care-free joy. These darkness dwellers seek to turn our joy into gloom to match the pitiful state in which they live. Surely, misery does, in fact, like company!

Life costs. So does freedom. If our land is to remain the land of the free then we must become vigilant. We must transcend self-interest and become more "otherly" concerned. This too is one of the costs of living in a post 9/11 world. We can only avoid these costs at our peril. One of the factors that made 9/11 inevitable was our refusal to pay the costs we have been eager to pay since that "day to remember." The bombing of the marine barracks in Beirut, the attack on the U.S.S. Cole, the bombing of the embassies in Africa—all these and many other acts of terrorism against us and our interests—should have alerted us that something was seriously wrong in the world, and that nothing short of a swift, sustained, and severe response was warranted. Rather than such a response, we retreated, for we were unwilling to pay the requisite costs. Now, those costs have been compounded.

Rule Number 18

The Game of Life Demands Listening to Everyone

Paying the costs of life is one lesson we must learn in our ascent from our status as a novice. When I consented to pay the costs of the game of golf, I took a giant leap, maybe not a giant one, but a leap nevertheless in my quest to become a golfer. The next step I had to take was learning to accept instruction and guidance from a peer. Juan was not a golf professional. However, he knew more about the game than I did. He had more experience than I. I found that the game went a great deal smoother when I listened to Juan. It is no different in life. There are others who have more knowledge and experience than we do. We should listen to them. It matters not their age, their sex, their race, or their position in life. We should be willing to listen to others who have knowledge and experience that we do not possess. We should not let what we think block the help that could come to us from those who know.

The marvelous story of Jack and the Beanstalk comes to mind. Jack's mother did not believe the story the young boy told her. She punished him and threw the beans out of the window. Her anger and disbelief were dissipated by the tremendous growth a few days later, a growth that led to riches beyond her wildest imagination. How foolish she must have felt when the beanstalk towered to the sky, and her son ascended it and returned with a king's riches. I doubt there has ever been a parent that at one time or another has not had to repent of having doubted a child. Wisdom, talent and good fortune are not respecters of persons, and yet they have been tossed to the wind by those who failed to realize that things are not always what they seem, and what we seek does not always come to us in the form we expect.

A further example is in order. During the waning years of Camelot, King Arthur learned of the legend of the Holy Grail. He became convinced that the wonders and majesty that were Camelot could be reclaimed if the lost Holy Grail could be found and brought to Camelot. So it was that he assembled his Knights of the Round Table and charged them with locating and bringing to Camelot the Holy Grail. Off they went into the world—they traveled to the farthest reaches of both the known and the unknown. Most of these brave and adventurous knights died along the way. Those that returned were broken and despondent and but a shell of their former selves.

In a final act of desperation, the once mighty king summoned his only son and charged him with this awesome task. If Camelot was to survive, it would be up to the son. The son, not wanting to fail at so critical a task, decided to approach his mission unlike his predecessors. Where they had traveled alone, he would assemble a mighty army. There is strength in numbers. That might be so, but he took no notice of the lessons of Jericho, that sometimes one can have too many numbers in one's company. Sometimes, our greatest challenges are best faced alone or with a few trusted companions.

The son gathered the remaining knights and all the able bodied men and young boys he could provide for. He now had his army. He chose a day consistent with the omens of the gods, and on that fateful day all the people of Camelot came out to wish him well. King Arthur, feeble and in ill health, mustered sufficient strength to consecrate his son and army to the task that lay before them. The priests sang their incantations and made offerings to the gods. Merlin concocted a special brew and enticed both son and army to drink it. All was ready. The trumpets strained to the distant winds. The drums beat out a cadence that was matched by the hoofs of mighty horses. "Open the castle gates," roared King Arthur, with all the strength he could muster.

The gates swung open and out into the blazing sun rode son and army. As the son came to the boundary separating castle and world, an old man appeared with a dirty and faded crochet sack slung over his shoulders. He was tall, thin, and disheveled. He motioned for the son to stop. This the son did by grabbing the reins of his horse and digging his boots into its side.

"What be the cause of this intrusion?" shouted the son, with a furor in his voice that shattered the silence of the nearby forest.

"How dare you demean this sacred occasion by your filthy presence! Had I the time, I would hang you by your toes and strip every remaining piece of skin from your pathetic body. Be gone!" the son roared.

The son again pulled the reins of his horse and kicked him in the right side. The horse reared up its head and in doing so tossed the old man out of the son's path. The son gave his horse a wry smile of approval and signaled the army forward. Off they marched into the distant horizon as the gates of Camelot closed for the final time. As the gates closed, a low flying eagle crashed into them and collapsed to the ground.

The army took no notice of these things. They were blinded by drink and singleness of purpose. On they rode until night overtook them and sleep beckoned them to that world of sweet repose. They slept and well they slept. All that is, except for the son. His sleep was disturbed by visions of the old man attempting to hand the sack on his back to the son. This dream soon became a nightmare and played repeatedly night after night in the mind of the son. After several days, he dispatched three of his best riders to fetch Merlin, the great sorcerer.

Within three days the riders returned with their quarry. Merlin beheld the disheveled son of his friend and king and invited him to relay his story. Merlin already knew what ailed the boy king. Like all great sorcerers and gods, Merlin knew without asking. He asked, then, not for his benefit but for that of his patient. There is great healing in the telling of what ails us. And so the boy king told Merlin the source of his pain.

When he had finished, the wise sage took hold of the boy's hand and looked softly into his eyes and said, "My son, that tethered old man had the very thing you seek in that sack strung over his shoulder."

The words of Merlin hit the young man like fiery darts from the fires of hell. He grabbed his chest, let out a ghastly yell and gave up the ghost of living. He fell silently into that long, cold sleep. Merlin could only pity the passing of the son of a friend and the end of that time and world that was Camelot.

The king's son erred in the opposite direction of Jack's mother. Both of them suffered because they rejected a blessing of heaven because they did not like the package in which it was dressed. For the mother it was youth. For the son of the king it was old age. How many of us are looking for things that are ever before us? However, we refuse to see and to acknowledge them because we do not like the packages in which they appear. When we learn to play it where it lies, we learn also to see beneath the package in which things are wrapped. We learn, as the Desiderata counsels, "Speak your truth quietly and clearly and listen to others, even the dull and ignorant; they too have their story." If only the king's son had listened.

"But what if I discover that the thing before me is not what I'm looking for?" you ask. Do not worry. Your life will be enriched by the experience and you will avoid being proven a fool like Jack's mother. Or worst, you will avoid the terrible fate of King Arthur's son and Camelot. Being disappointed is an acceptable cost for playing it where it lies. Throwing away the chance or love of a lifetime is an unacceptable cost.

Jack's mother and King Arthur's son were novices. Unfortunately, neither of them was able to progress beyond that state of existence. One thing to the credit of both of these tragic figures is that both of them tried. They both hung in there despite the odds. There are many novices who refuse to do this. And so we say that Jack's mother and the son of the great king were tragic figures because they tried. Those novices who do not try are not tragic figures—they are just pitiful.

Rule Number 19
"Don't Go Gently Into That Good Night"

These are misguided souls who say to hell with the game of life. These are the ones who jump off bridges, "blow their brains out," overdose on drugs and inflict all manners of death upon themselves. They reach a point where they think the costs of staying in the game of life are too great. The burdens are too heavy. The pain is unbearable. Oh, a million and one reasons they give for ending their lives before they have begun or at the twilight of what could truly be their golden years. These are novices at the game of life who do not seek further growth. They give up any hope of graduating to a higher class.

Albert Camus, in his classic, The Myth of Sisyphus, has done what I consider to be the best analysis of the mind of the intentional suicide. I refer you to that marvelous work for erudition of this complex subject. I will share but a few of his pearls of wisdom here.

There is one final category of novices worth mentioning here. That is the unintentional suicide. A story from the book of life is illustrative of the point I wish to make here. The story is told of a woman who had been raised in a church which taught the importance of "waiting on the Lord." It so happened that one day during a torrential rainstorm, it began to flood in her city. She watched as the waters began to rise.

"Come, lady, can't you see the waters are rising? We have to abandon our homes and move to higher ground," called out her neighbors who were vacating the neighborhood.

"Go ahead. I'm waiting on the Lord. The Lord will make a way for me," said the lady, and so she remained.

The waters continued to rise and began to creep into her house. She heard a loud noise and went outside, where the sheriff was in a boat with a bull horn. He called to her to let him help her into the boat to evacuate before the waters rose any higher.

"Don't worry about me. I'm waiting on the Lord. I'll be all right," she said. She closed the door as the sheriff continued on his way in search of others. Before leaving, he called out to her several more times. The sound of the rising tides was the only response.

The waters continued to rise. The sound of the sheriff's boat had hardly faded into the distance when the waters burst through the lady's front door with a sound that would have raised the dead were the ground not covered in an ocean of water. The lady ran upstairs and crawled out onto the roof of her house.

A helicopter happened by. Its pilot saw the lady and hovered over her house. A basket descended as a passenger called out to the lady to jump into the basket. Again, as she had several times before, the lady declined. She repeated her refrain of waiting on the Lord.

Meanwhile, the waters continued to rise. The occupants of the helicopter could only look on in horror and bewilderment as the waters swallowed the house and the lady.

The lady must have been more holy than she was foolish. For she opened her eyes in Heaven. There, not content to have reached the majesty of the throne of grace, she made her way to the Trinitarian scepter, where she inquired of her god, "God, I waited for you. Why didn't you ever come?"

God, ever patient with fools and drunks, looked upon the lady with eyes of love and said gently, "My child, I came to you in three different persons and you refused me each time!"[19] The lady could only slip away in silence. She realized that she had failed to play it where it lies.

I suppose that there have been many times that messengers of God have come to us, and we have refused to listen because we did not like the clothes they were wearing or the form in which they appeared. Had God a head, he would no doubt find it constantly turning in disgust and sheer amazement that we would so readily squander the fantastic life He gives to us. Like the lady who could not recognize the appearance of God, we commit suicide unintentionally. We close the annals of history on kingdoms, give up the gift of life, and cause untold misery and tragedies because we are novices who never grow up and learn to appreciate life in all its many splendors. We form images and ideas of how the world ought to look, then we live our lives far below the abundant life we could enjoy were we to just open up to life and let go of our prejudices and entertain, even if for a fleeting moment, the idea that life could be other than we suppose.

This point, that life can be other than we suppose, was driven home to me during my years in seminary. Part of my training was what is called clinical pastoral education—an unpaid internship at a local nonprofit institution or church. Mine was performed at the VA Hospital in Dallas. One day I took advantage of the only monetary benefit I received for six weeks of work—lunch for a dollar. I took a dollar out of my wallet and paid for lunch. Later that day, I went to the commissary to purchase a pair of socks and some other items for a patient who was being released from the hospital that day. When I arrived at the check out, I reached for my wallet. It was gone. I set the items down and went to the cafeteria, where I hoped to find my wallet. It was not there. I became upset, then incensed. I kept telling the manager repeatedly how certain I was that I had left my wallet there, for I had extracted a dollar from it with which to pay for lunch. Still, the wallet did not appear. I accused the manager and her employees of dishonesty and stormed out.

Later that evening, when my shift was over, I left, still angry, and went to my car for the drive home. As soon as I got into my vehicle I saw it. There in the console was my wallet. "How did that get there," I asked the eternal verities. I was about to accuse the manager of the cafeteria or one of her employees of placing the wallet there when a rush of enlightenment seized me. I experienced what Gestalt therapists call an "a-ha moment."

I then remembered that on my way to work that morning, I had stopped at a traffic light, and there was a young man selling apples. I had taken my wallet out to buy a few. The light had changed before I had time to return my wallet to my back pocket, and so I had placed it on the console, expecting to retrieve it upon arriving at work. However when I arrived at work, I had to drive around to find a parking place, and this made me late. So, once having found a place to park, I jumped out of my car and ran to work. I had forgotten my wallet.

I must have placed the change in my shirt pocket instead of in my wallet, and that explained how I was able to pay for my lunch. I felt shame and disgust at this discovery. I was sure, no, I was certain that I had had my wallet at lunch. I would have staked my life on my belief that I had my wallet when I paid for lunch. And yet, I was wrong. My senses had failed me. My power of reasoning had failed me. The world was other than I supposed. Needless to say, the next day I took all my courage and humility to apologize to the manager and her employees.[20]

Sometimes, life is other than we suppose. It is other than we know or think it to be. Is not that all the more reason to hang in there? Ought not the uncertainty of life and our failure to always fully comprehend life reason enough for us to keep playing the game? We can be so sure, so convinced, and yet, so wrong. We can truly believe that we are at the end of our rope when suddenly it seems to grow another length, or someone comes along and throws us another line. We can think that life has gotten on our last nerve, and then we experience another firing of nerves we did not know we had. No matter how we perceive life, there is always the possibility that something other than we perceive will emerge. Life is filled with wondrous adventures and what many call miracles.

Oh, dear reader, are you a novice? Are you too giving up on the game of life, either intentionally or unintentionally? Have you considered that we may, in fact, have only "One Life to Live"?

In faith, we declare that there is a Heaven waiting to receive us. In sheer hope we opine that Nirvana exists. But what if we are wrong? What if, despite the wisdom of the ages, the hope of all humankind, the dreams and aspirations of countless people—both wise and foolish, there is nothing beyond this life? No, not even darkness for that would require some kind of consciousness to perceive it. Should we not make the most of this life for it is the only one of which we can be sure. All the scriptures, all the philosophies, even John Edwards, Edgar Cayce, Shirley McClain and Sylvia Browne; all these have failed to come forward with sufficient credible evidence to convince us that there is a life beyond this one or a side other than this one. No matter where we start, be it scripture, philosopher, or spiritualist, it always comes down to faith. Reason might begin the sentence but faith always ends it. If the case of the afterlife was submitted to a jury, they would remain hopelessly deadlocked. If to a judge, the judge would have to dismiss the case for lack of evidence. Like King Agrippa, the judge would say in hope that he/she is "almost persuaded." Nevertheless, the judge would be forced by the rules of law to dismiss the case and let the parties continue to argue before the court of public hope and the halls of faith. Oh, we hope that there is life after this one. We believe that there is. We need there to be. But what, my friend, if there is not?

Ought we to live life to the fullest? Even if there is a life to come after this one, does it not behoove us to live as if there is not? Ought we not to live life fully and completely and morally, and where it lies, so that we can gain the victory in this life. And then if there is no other life, we would have received our reward, and if there is another life we would have received a double portion?

I am not suggesting that we all run to the betting window and accept Pascal's wager. For doing so is to live in the default margins of life. We are not cowards looking to hedge our bets. We are people who play it where it lies and in doing so we act intentionally and forcefully and accept responsibility for our choices and actions.

Because we can never know for sure whether or not there is an afterlife, a heaven or a hell, a Nirvana or a paradise, this should be cause for us to be less impatient with those who hold beliefs contrary to our own, or those who hold no beliefs at all. Would not many of the conflicts in the world cease immediately if more people would take hold of what we say here? Oh, the joy that would overcome the world if those who believe themselves to be repositories of "truth" could but realize that, at best, they have but a great hope. A mighty and at times persuasive hope, but just a hope nevertheless. Why give up this life for a mere hope—even if it is a powerful hope?

Even I, as the gloom of the day gives way to night, as the cool day becomes the cold night, I thank "whatever gods may be" for this opportunity to live. I too hope. I too have faith. No matter how cold it gets, how heavy the gloom presses about me, life with all its drudgery, with all its pains and sufferings, is always worth living. I still desire to sail among the clouds and to swim to the distant horizon. Yet, as I look at my sleeping wife and the smile into which her lips are curved, as I reflect on the joys that are my children and the challenges presented by my students, I am content to be earthbound for a while longer. Even though the burden of living gets heavy and the costs of life are exorbitant, I choose to stay in the game. After all, "a winner never quits and a quitter never wins." If I do not win, may my exit be met with the roar of the crowd applauding my efforts and shouting to high heaven: "There goes a man who played it where it lies with dignity and honor and grace!"

6

THE CHAPERONED

In the previous chapter, we encountered some metaphysical difficulty. One of the reasons I have always struggled with notions of metaphysical realities is that I have been able to give an account of certain epistemological dispositions without resort to metaphysics. And even though I want very much to believe in such notions, I cannot deny the wisdom that comes to me from the ancients in a way that does not implicate metaphysics.

As I ponder those things to which metaphysics have oftentimes been applied, it becomes ever clearer to me that there is within humans a common ocean of experiences, and I can access the experiences within my genetic heritage which have had such encounters and, in so doing, make those experiences my own. This may account for *deja vu* experiences in which people claim to experience something unknown to them—one comes to a place and suddenly one gets the feeling one has been there before. However, the person has never been to that place or that country. How can we account for this?

Typically, we must resort to some system of metaphysics or extrasensory perception to give an account of such experiences. Not so with me. I am of the opinion that the time will come when scientists will discover that within the genetic code is a strain of genes that retain the memories of countless numbers of persons who have gone on before us and who have bequeathed to us a part of their memories. When we go to a place to which we have never been and the place seems familiar to us, it is because someone who lived before us either went there or to a place very similar to it, and the memory of that experience is recorded in our genetic memory bank.

A similar explanation can account for the testimonies of those who claim to have lived previous lives and who can give convincing reports of the life and times of bygone eras. Assuming such accounts can be verified and the reporter is not recalling something read in a book or seen on television or at the movies or received from some other source, then it is because such persons have been able to recover the memories of those who appear in their genetic genealogy. Hence, mind travel—if there is any validity to the questionable enterprise—is not going somewhere I have been before; nor is it the recovery of a previous life I have lived. Mind travel is nothing more than a borrowed memory. It is like the image that remains on the television screen for a fleeting second when one turns off the set. If one could capture those images and retain them in a device (like the innovative Tivo), it would be much like the way our genetic system works. Certain memories are so powerful that they blaze a path or leave an imprint in the genetic code of the person who has such memorable encounters, and these are passed on to subsequent generations in their genetic stream. That is why two people seldom have the same *deja vu* or related experience at the same time, although this does happen sometimes among persons who are related.

Sylvia Browne gives a similar account for why we can sense the presence of people who have died and passed on to the other side. She explains that the person had some type of traumatic event and, as a result, left a psychic imprint that we can sense. For Sylvia, the imprint is not within us—it is within the material universe. It is restricted to a particular place and is reenacted repeatedly—much like when one of those old scratched vinyl records gets stuck and replays the same melody again. I applaud Sylvia's insight. Though I would not go so far as to say the departed person has passed on to the other side, for Sylvia means that the person continues on in some type of spiritual form. That moves us back to metaphysics, and, at this juncture, I do not wish to go there, as the young people would say.

I had a student relate to me that she was a Filipino American. Her parents were Filipinos, but she was born in America. During her first trip to the Philippines, she met a man at the airport who moved toward her but who did not speak. Later, while reviewing the photo albums of her grandmother, she saw a photo that appeared familiar. She asked her grandmother who the man in the photo was. Her grandmother explained that was her grandfather, who had been dead for a number of years. "But grandmother," she protested. "I saw that man at the airport!"

When I questioned the student, she could not furnish any further details of the encounter. It would seem that Sylvia's analysis would not help us here because we cannot tell what type of traumatic event might have triggered the leaving of such an imprint, or that any degree of trauma had occurred with the grandfather at the airport. The man did not seem to be in any type of distress. The student said he had smiled. It would have been fascinating had I been able to question the grandmother as to whether or not the grandfather had any relationship with the airport. Moreover, it might be helpful to question the mother to determine whether she had encountered her father at the airport or whether her husband had. Of course, caution should be exercised here, for we are not always aware of our past memories. We can have many experiences that we cannot recall at any given moment, for they have receded to the deepest storage area of our subconscious mind.

Notwithstanding our inability to proceed with Sylvia's methodology, we can perhaps more readily explain this encounter under the vision I am sharing here. One of the keys to "unpacking" such encounters is to ask what kind of clothes the ghost was wearing. I have never received a report of a ghostly encounter in which the ghost was naked. Ghosts appear to be quite modest! All the reports I have received involved ghosts wearing clothes. And the reporters could not give an account of why the ghost was wearing clothes.

Are clothes eternal? Do they too survive the transition to the other side and thus reappear as spiritual clothes? Do "all good" clothes "go to heaven"? The notion is too absurd to entertain. I did have one student say that ghosts appear in a form we can recognize and feel comfortable with. However, that ascribes to ghosts a power that Durkheim denies they possess, and such a notion seems nonsensical at best. A ghost wearing clothes cannot be a traveler from across that great divide. Perhaps that is why when the women arrived at the grave of Jesus they found only his burial clothes. What need has spirit of clothes?

I am convinced that the reason ghosts appear in clothes is because the encounter is a memory or an imprint. My student who traveled to the Philippines probably experienced an encounter that her mother or grandmother had once experienced, and that encounter was stored in her genetic memory bank. Traveling to the Philippines, with all the anxiety, excitement, and stress associated with going home for the first time, triggered the release of a stored memory. Or, her grandfather spent some memorable times at the airport and imprinted an image that is frozen there like the fleeting image on a television screen.

It is like looking at the sun. You glance up at the sun for a few seconds and turn away. You now see the sun in whatever you see for the next few seconds or minutes. Surely, you would not think yourself to have captured the sun. You have acquired an imprint of the sun on the television screen of your sense perceptions, and that imprint will last a few seconds after you turn the screen off (stop looking at the sun). It is like that image that makes the rounds of the Internet. You are instructed to look at the image then to close your eyes. For a few seconds or minutes, you see the image of Jesus Christ. Have you peered into the metaphysical heaven? Have you captured Jesus Christ? Of course not! You have but imprinted an image on the television screen of your sense perceptions. See how quickly it fades. Moreover, I doubt a person from another country who has not been indoctrinated with ideas about Jesus Christ would see him as a result of looking at the image. For how could such a person identify someone of whom he/she had no knowledge? It is like asking a person to pick a suspect out of a police line-up when the person never saw the suspect before.

Sylvia's insight can, however, help us to understand why some people, such as the Native Americans and certain tribes in West Africa, have always found certain places occupied by the spirits of deceased loved ones. It may be that the religions of these people are nothing more than interpretations of encounters with imprints. What we call ghosts may be nothing more than a frozen image on the television screen of life. That image will soon dissipate as does the image on our television screen. Might this account for why we can not find the burning bush and empty tomb today?

"When," you ask, is soon? Remember, that time is a human invention. The universe has no cognizance of this human construct. What seems like decades to us would be nothing more than a fraction of a second to the universe. That is, if we read the universal text as poetry and not as prose.

One final word on this matter and this is to my Christian friends. It is amazing that so many Christians appear quite happily on the John Edwards' show and related venues, in which they claim to interact with persons who have crossed over to the other side. They do this notwithstanding the parable Jesus told of Lazarus and the rich man, in which the rich man asks Lazarus to go to his brothers who were then still alive. Abraham responds that there can be no communication between the other side and this world. Or recall that incisive investigator, philosopher and physician, William James, who sat with paper and pen outside the door of his dying spiritualist friend who had promised to deliver a message to James, who wanted so much to receive the message as soon as the friend crossed over to the other side. James waited and waited but there was only silence.

And there was Ms. Cayce, to whom the "Sleeping Prophet," Edgar Cayce, made a similar promise. Despite her love for her husband and her belief in his gifts, she too received only silence.

Then, there is the great Houdini, who found so many ways to escape the chains and locks of this world but could not escape the final lock of death. He too promised a word from beyond. All his anxious fans received was silence. How, then, can Christians persist in believing something that is directly contradicted by their Lord and Savior? I wonder if Professor Phillips has some of my Christian friends in mind when writing his book on friendly fire. I shall read it with interest to see if I can identify any of them. God forbid that I should be accounted among that work.

We have had to take what might appear to some as a lengthy detour in these opening observations to place into proper focus the final response to "playing it where it lies." That is because this last category of strayers from the path seems to appeal to metaphysical powers to enable their dependency and to justify their refusal to take responsibility for their own lives. But first, a biographical interlude is needed to sharpen our gaze.

Rule Number 20
Always Be Willing to Pay for the Benefits You Enjoy

I was married for the first time at the age of 18 to a wonderful young lady[21] from Detroit, Michigan, whom I had met during a visit there in the summer of 1969. We relocated back to Texas. This was after my graduation from the job corps, with a certificate in office administration and a general equivalency diploma. Initially, after my graduation, I had enrolled at the local junior college. However, hardly a month had gone by when I was kicked out. I had run afoul of a state law that provided that if a student dropped out of school and obtained a general equivalency diploma, that student could not enroll in college until after the student's high school class has graduated. It was after being kicked out of college that I had gone to Detroit.

Now that I was back at home, I obtained a very good job with the postal service. A year later, I received the standard greeting from Uncle Sam, saying how much he needed me in the Army. My wife persuaded me to go to Canada in an attempt to avoid going to

Vietnam. Without any hesitation, I accepted her persuasion, and we departed Fort Worth. Our plan was to stop over in Detroit, where I would obtain a job with her father at the Chrysler-McGraw Glass Plant for a few months, and then we would head on to Canada. We traveled by Greyhound bus.

Prior to reaching our destination, we stopped at a restaurant and there was a college student at the restaurant reading a book on Aristotle. The book appeared familiar to me, though I had never even heard of Aristotle. I had never in my life read a book on philosophy. And yet, here I was, attracted to a book on Aristotle.

I asked the student to allow me to look at the book for a moment. Without thinking, I turned to a section on Socrates—the very section where Socrates was discussing his refusal to consent to being exiled: For how can a man who has been kicked out of his own country be worthy of living in the country of others?

Socrates' question struck me with the force of a hurricane. Here I was, for all practical purposes, a fugitive from justice. I was leaving my own country—because I was unwilling to serve in its military—to go live in a country where I would enjoy the service of others. How could I live in a country, and enfold myself in its arms of protection, and take advantage of my access to its vault of opportunities, and yet refuse to serve that country? It was much like the wealthy person who gives up all her riches to take up a begging bowl. How can I claim enlightenment when I am dependent upon others having the very things I have given up? My Christian friends make so much out of

Jesus' presumed poverty. They seem to overlook the fact he had a treasurer among the apostles.

I was silent the remainder of the way to Detroit. How could I explain what had just happened to me? In fact, this event has continued to disturb me until I sat down to write this work for your edification. It is in writing this work that I have finally come to understand what was happening to me. Writing is very therapeutic. No doubt, this encounter with Socrates can be explained by my vision—someone in my genetic stream either encountered the real Socrates or read about him. I was accessing the memory of that encounter.

At any rate, whatever the source of this encounter with Socrates, the next day after arriving in Detroit, I went to the Army recruiting station and signed up for the Army. Sure, it would mean serving three years instead of two, but at least it would keep me out of Vietnam. My wife was furious. So furious that, while I went off to the Army, she went to the arms of another man.

By joining the Army, I was able to select the occupational specialty I wanted. I chose that of being a clerk. After basic and advanced training and leadership school, I was stationed in Germany, where I served for six months before getting new orders to go to Vietnam. Suddenly, my plan was falling to pieces. For in Vietnam, I was no longer a clerk but an infantryman. I had joined the Army to avoid combat and Vietnam, and now I faced them both. "Life is what happens ..."

I did not have the time to consult with a contracts attorney to determine if the Army had violated our contract. Nor could I, as John Wayne does in the movie, "The Green Berets," march into my commander's office and say, "I joined this outfit and now I quit!" All I could do was to obey this new directive.

I was in Vietnam for about six months when President Nixon announced his Vietnamization program, in which American forces were being moved behind the lines, and the forces of South Vietnam were being moved to the front lines. As a result, Nixon commanded that American troops in Vietnam be reduced, and the Army concocted several schemes to comply. One of those was an early out if one agreed to serve the remaining of one's time in the active reserves. That is the strategy I took. Soon, I was out of the Army. I had served 20 months—less than I was obligated to serve and less than I would have served had I been drafted. Although I had taken a serendipitous route, I was now where I intended to be. And this had been accomplished by playing it where it lies. This brings us to the point to which this long introduction has been moving.

During my tenure in the active reserves, our reserve unit was ordered to provide traffic control and other services for the Colonial Invitational Golf Tournament. To compensate our unit for these services, Colonial agreed to allow us to play golf at this prestigious course for one full day. Truly it was a unique and enjoyable experience to play golf on this course that I could never afford. I was shocked, however; when we arrived at the course and were told we would have chaperones! The purpose of these was supposedly to show us around the course, but they were also to guard against our damaging the golf course. This was made clear to me when I was asked to take off my golf shoes and put on a pair provided by the pro shop because the spikes on my shoes were too big and they were causing too many divots in the course grounds. Having a chaperone truly deflated the balloon of our enjoyment. It is much akin to having a chaperone at one's high school prom.

Rule Number 21
Avoid Being Chaperoned

The idea of a chaperone is repugnant to a free thinking, responsible individual. We want to make our own decisions, go where we want to go, do what we want to do. Even when we lament the weight of having always to make our own decisions and bear the responsibility for them, as I do in the previous chapter, we do not wish to turn that task over to others. Ask anyone who has ever had a guardian appointed for him/her. Inquire at any local nursing home how the residents feel having their lives planned and directed by others. Nevertheless, there are many people for whom a chaperone is necessary. Not only those who may be physically or mentally impaired, but those who cannot conform themselves to the rules of the game. "One Flew Over the Cuckoo's Nest" is a powerful dramatization of this point, although the movie takes the point to its tragic extreme.

When I allowed my former wife to make the decision for me to go to Canada, I consented to her being my chaperone. Had I gone to Canada, my life would have been placed in the hands of others upon whom I would have had to rely for subsistence and protection from discovery and arrest. Soon, I would have found myself living in the default area of life, where I had lost all intentionality.

This is the final response to playing it where it lies. It is that place at which so many people abandon the game and give their lives over to the control of others or something else. A great many alcoholics and drug addicts fit into this category. We say that people do drugs, but in actuality, it is the drug doing the person.

This idea of giving our lives over to the control of others is reflected in the ancient wisdom of the Spinhx. You recall that to pass the way of the Spinhx one had to answer the following riddle:

What walks on four legs in the morning, two in the afternoon, three in the evening and has to be carried at night?[22]

The answer is man: he crawls at birth, then walks on two legs, then three in old age when he uses a cane, and finally he has to be carried when he becomes totally disabled and dies. If we add metaphysics, then the man has to be carried when he dies as that golden Negro hymnal says, "Swing low, sweet chariot, comin for to carry me home!" When Lazarus dies, he does not go to Abraham's bosom; he has to be carried there. This idea is highlighted in the marvelous movie, "Ghost," where either agents of darkness or agents of light come to carry one to one's eternal destination. I am quite willing to give myself over to a chaperone to carry me across that great divide, though we ought to heed the warning of Chris De Burgh that we "Don't pay the ferryman until he gets you to the other side." Until then, I choose to play it where it lies by living life intentionally and by making choices and accepting responsibility for the choices I make.

Night has come for too many of those around us. They have to be carried even though there is nothing wrong with their limbs. The people who overpopulate our penal institutions can be counted here. The irony of these institutions is that they do such a good job of chaperoning that inmates who are released find it difficult to live on their own, and so they work their way back into prison. People on probation and parole also give evidence of the wisdom we advocate here. Homeless people are additional proof. These people have dropped out of the game because they played into an unplayable lie and lacked the tools and/or knowledge to move beyond the hazard. Their system of decision making shut down on them. Their power-house of choice making blew a fuse. And so they sat down on the ground with their head hid in their hands and waited for someone to come along and chaperone them. It made no difference to them who fulfilled that role.

Yes, there are far too many people who are unwilling to make choices, and who fall into the default dimensions of life. Not only do such people refuse to make intentional choices about their life, they do not wish to play the game. They resign and just let whatever happens happen. Flannery O'Connor had such people in mind when she penned that tragic tale, "A Good Man Is Hard to Find." The story is that of a family out on a Sunday drive. The father/husband brings along his grandmother, who begins to give directions. The wife attempts to intervene and suggests that those directions are faulty. The husband refuses to listen and even as it is clear to him that they are getting lost, he refuses to take control of their journey and politely remind the grandmother that a car has only one steering wheel. Instead, he allows her to give faulty directions which he follows until they are hopelessly lost, and the automobile breaks down.

That is not the end of the story. How I wish it were. For soon a group of men appear on the scene, and the grandmother announces that they are good men, and she knew they would come to the rescue. Again, the husband/father does not object. He remains silent as the men take the children and the rest of the family, and finally him, off one by one and kill them. You see, fair reader, these men had just escaped from a mental institution.

Were there not a number of points at which this tragedy could have been averted? Had the husband/father but stayed in the game rather than abandon himself to the tradition of the elders.

Or reflect for a moment on the wisdom of Camus in his short story, "The Guest." A rebel who has been injured in the revolution stumbles across a school house, where a lone teacher nurses him back to health. When he is able to move on his own, the teacher takes him behind the school house and points out two roads: one leading to freedom and the other leading to prison and death. The teacher turns and heads back to resume his duties as a teacher. Just prior to reaching the schoolhouse, the teacher pauses and turns to check on his patient. What a sight he beheld. The patient was walking merrily up the road leading to prison and death. When the teacher returns to his classroom, someone has written upon the chalkboard the teacher is going to die for having killed the comrade of those left behind.

Part of the lesson Camus wants to teach us is that the patient needed a chaperone, and the teacher refused to become one. There is a good reason why the teacher chose to decline a position so many others are willing to accept. When one consents to be a chaperone, one gives up some of the freedom to be all that one can be, for one has taken on weight that will keep one from sailing to the highest heights. And what if others blame us for the death of the one for whom we refused to act as chaperone? We stand our ground and accept the risk. There is always risk when we choose to play it where it lies.

In closing, it is helpful for us to make special note of the wide variance between a chaperone and a coach. That difference has been made quite clear to me during my sojourn in the Philippines. My Filipino wife, not possessing the meek and submissive nature I had been told Asian women possess, has at times taken me literally by the hand and directed me where to go. She has said to me constantly, "Watch your head!" "Be careful!" She has told me when to go to bed, when to wake up, when to eat and most of the times what to eat. There have been times when she has spoon fed me. Yet, in all these things, she has explained to me how and why these were the best things for me at that moment. And I, with all my earned degrees, my fierce independence, and my vast experiences, could do no more than to submit to her authority.

Yet, this is not the evening of my life. Consequently, I am not being chaperoned by my wife. Quite the contrary, this is the dawn of a new day for me. It is a day that is mediated by the coaching of my lovely wife. This is a time of beginning and not ending. For it has been during this journey through the Philippines that I have discovered the path I now commend to you. A chaperone makes decisions for you. A coach assists you in making your own decisions.

Take the following experience as evidence of the light that has come into my life. A lady who is seventy years of age walked over an hour from her farm in the mountains to hear me speak. I was so impressed that I vowed to visit her before my departure. I made good on my promise a week later. I took a taxi for an hour, then the rest of the way had to be negotiated on foot. It took a little under an hour to reach her humble abode. While there, I witnessed a life I have only heard of and read about. There was no running water, no electricity, nor was there any plumbing or outhouse.

I watched as her brother and farm hand gathered several chickens, and some other women slit their throats and held them until the blood drained from their bodies and they stopped shaking. Then, the lifeless chickens were handed over to a farmhand who had started a fire over which he placed a cast iron skillet filled with water. Once the water started boiling, he placed a chicken in it, turned it over several times, and then handed it to another woman who defeathered it. After all the chickens were defeathered, they were held over the open fire for several minutes and rubbed with salt, and some were sent into the house to be cut off and made into debulo—a Filipino delicacy—and the remaining chickens were roasted over the fire, using spits made of bamboo. For a brief moment, I vowed never to eat another chicken.

However, once the table was set, the aroma and color of the food were too enticing to pass up. I dug in to what was truly a most sumptuous meal. Following the meal and a period of rest, it was time to depart. I wondered what I could give this woman to express my deep appreciation for the life she had given me and for the deep and profound joy I now felt. She asked if I would pray for her. I consented and asked her if she needed anything in particular. She said she wanted chickens. I was astounded by her request. I questioned her to make sure I had not misunderstood. Again she said chickens. She explained in her broken dialect, which my wife interpreted, that a recent famine had wiped out most of her chickens.

Here we were an hour from the nearest road up in the mountains. And this seventy year-old woman did not desire electricity, running water, a restroom, a refrigerator, a microwave, a television or any of the myriad of things we in the United States think we cannot live without. All she wanted were more chickens! How have we come so far away from the simple things of life? Will we ever recover them?

Tears welled up in my eyes as I thought of how complex and demanding we have made our lives, and how we have surrounded our lives with things, and indoctrinated our children with our disease so that they, too, do not believe they can make it without a cell phone and the latest technological gadget. What kind of a world have we created, in which so many young people can strip down a computer and reassemble it, but cannot recite the Pledge of Allegiance from memory and do not know the preamble to the United States Constitution?

With these thoughts and many others whizzing through my mind, I prayed to the God whose existence I said earlier was still in doubt. I prayed to that ultimate metaphysical reality, notwithstanding my doubts, then and now, as to whether there is any such thing beyond the mental confines of humans. Yes, I prayed for this woman and for myself and for my children and for you and for your children. And I prayed for chickens.

7

WINNING

Play it where it lies. That is the battle cry we have raised to a humanity that has lost its way. Like the *cri de coeur* of the Texas revolutionaries, which reverberated throughout the land of Tejas, "Remember the Alamo," our proclamation here is intended to stir our hearts and minds to action that we might salvage this game and turn a certain loss into a definite win.

No doubt, you, my good and faithful readers, are wondering just what it is that we mean by winning. A bumper sticker displays the message, "He who dies with the most toys win." Another one counsels, "He who wins the rat race is still a rat!" Somewhere between or beyond these two extremes lies our answer.

For instance, in a marvelous quote on the definition of success, Ralph Waldo Emerson is said to have written:

To laugh often and much;
To win the respect of intelligent people and the affection of
    children;
To earn the appreciation of honest critics and endure the betrayal of
    false friends;
To appreciate beauty, to find the best in others;
To leave the world a bit better, whether by a healthy child, a garden
    patch or a redeemed social condition;
To know even one life has breathed easier because you have lived.
This is to have succeeded.

—inaccurately attributed to Ralph Waldo Emerson[23]

As beautiful as the foregoing quotation is, whether Emerson is the
author or not, the elements of success enumerated there will not
suffice here. A person can do all those marvelous things and still not
win the crown of victory offered by the instant path. The reason is
simply that one may walk like a duck and talk like a duck and even
quack like a duck and yet not be a duck but just a good imitation.

It is a false hope to proclaim that success in life is all about
externalities. Success in life is also about the internal nature of a
person. We have said already, in golf, the player with the lowest
score wins. I am of the opinion that in the game of life, the person
with the lowest score also wins. This lowest score is achieved not
only by doing, but by being as well. In these remaining pages, I hope
to make clear what I mean by the lowest score.

First, we revisit our bumper stickers. Does he or she who dies
with the most toys win? One of my favorite cities to visit in the entire
world is Las Vegas. The reason is that I can visit so much of the
world just by traversing "the strip." There is Paris, England, Egypt,

Rome, New York, and others. I can retreat into the past or be projected far into the future. I can live in luxury for a few dollars a day or live the life of a gypsy. Among all that this grand city has to offer, the Luxor hotel and casino is among the very finest. That is because it captures all that was magnificent and glorious about ancient Egypt. The Luxor Hotel and Casino is also one of only two human made artifacts on earth that can be seen from space—the other being the Great Wall of China.

Within the confines of the Luxor are many of the original (and a great many copies) treasures of the pharaohs. You recall that the pharaohs were among the first to advocate that he who died with the most toys win. And so they invested much of their country's resources and human power into building awesome pyramids that were loaded with treasures and attendants and other things that they would need in the next life. I wonder what they would make of the fact that those treasures are now in Las Vegas and other museums and residences and hotels around the world. The toys that the pharaohs died with are now being enjoyed by others. In what sense then did the pharaohs win? And if you say they won, what was the nature of their winnings?

What the pharaohs considered a chamber of transition was nothing more than a grand cold and final resting place that would yield up its treasure to thief and archaeologist alike. I do not deny the grand nature of the wonders of the pyramids. They are remarkable achievements in the annals of human existence. They reflect much of the genius that is resident in humans. They also represent monuments to the failed hopes of humans who hoped their toys would be delivered into whatever life follows this one. It is said that "dead men tell no lies." To that we can add, neither does the grave.

For the graves of those ancient human gods tell us that what was thought to be needed in the world to come remained in the grave until removed by succeeding generations. The graves tell us that if the pharaohs did find their way to another dimension, the so-called other side, then their stuff did not follow them. Again, my doubts expressed earlier about ghosts return. How can a ghost appear in clothes? The graves reveal that such things deteriorate or remain confined to the material world. How is a ghost able to resurrect clothes? Is there a metaphysical transition for clothes? The grave suggests there is not.

Thus, what ever winning means, it cannot mean the accumulation of things. For no matter how magical our lives have been, we still cannot take our stuff with us as Shelly reminds us:

Ozymandias

I MET a Traveler from an antique land,
Who said, "Two vast and trunkless legs of stone
Stand in the desart. Near them, on the sand,
Half sunk, a shattered visage lies, whose frown,
And wrinkled lip, and sneer of cold command,
Tell that its sculptor well those passions read,
Which yet survive, stamped on these lifeless things,
The hand that mocked them and the heart that fed:
And on the pedestal these words appear:
"My name is OZYMANDIAS, King of Kings."
Look on my works ye Mighty, and despair!
No thing beside remains. Round the decay
Of that Colossal Wreck, boundless and bare,
The lone and level sands stretch far away.[24]

Winning then, has to do not with the accumulation of things but rather with the accumulation of something less. That something is karma.

There is a fundamental law of nature that all our actions and inactions, our thoughts and feelings, our wants and desires, have implications of karma. We either accumulate negative karma that weighs us down or we accumulate positive karma that allows us to sail among the stars. Karma attaches to our soul, and when we incur too much negative karma, we become weighted down and cannot move forward or upward. It may be that the engrams that are the targets of L. Ron Hubbard's "clearing" process are nothing more than the residue of negative karma.

When I was a little boy, one of my favorite comic strip characters was the Silver Surfer. I eagerly waited for each new edition to see in what far away place in the galaxy the Silver Surfer would find adventure. I began to imagine, without any religious persuasion, that the Silver Surfer was a metaphor for how it is with our lives. That is, the less baggage we possess, the higher we can sail among the clouds, and then, with the stars, after the soul is released from the body.

As I grew older and commenced my studies, the concept of karma became clear to me, and I came to understand it as a universal principle. We say, "What goes around comes around." The Wiccans have a principle: the bad one does always returns to one threefold. Jesus said one reaps what one sows. An old African proverb says "Ashes fly back in the face of him who throws them."

These sayings reflect different names for the same universal principle—karma. Karma is a principle that governs our lives every millisecond of our existence. We cannot escape its effect. Take for instance, the young lady who kept saying she was sorry to the homeless man embedded in her automobile windshield. Like so many others among us, she thought that saying she was sorry would somehow lessen the weight of her crimes. She thought that saying she was sorry would erase her deficits from the book of universal liability. She discovered at her trial how wrong she was.

So it is with people everywhere who think that saying those two words—"I'm sorry"—will ameliorate the karma of their negative actions. It does not and will not. This is all the more reason why the path we choose is of such critical importance. For the path I am advocating will help one to avoid having to say those meaningless words. As the late William Ward said, "Love means never having to say I'm sorry." Likewise, obeying the rules of Play It Where It Lies means experiencing ever fewer times when one will have to resort to meaningless expressions.

Like little children who soon must learn that saying "I take it back" has no effect on the hurt they have caused, we must acknowledge that there are no incantations to suspend the operation of karma. One should think before one acts to avoid causing someone else pain and grief. Life is not like a game of jacks. When one throws the jacks and is not satisfied with the lay of the jacks, one can not shout, "Overs" and throw the jacks again. Life does not allow for "overs." Once the words are said or the deed is done, one's karma debt is recorded in that cosmic ledger book. No incantation can erase that debt. As a recent case study affirms, the debt will have to be paid.

Sara Jane Olson was the epitome of what has become known in the United States as a "soccer mom." She lived in St. Paul, Minnesota, where she was married to a doctor and was the proud parent of three beautiful and active daughters. Sarah acted in Community Theater and volunteered for many community projects.

One can imagine her shock when one day while driving her minivan she was pulled over by the police and members of the FBI. Sara's past, which she thought was long lost and forgotten, had suddenly caught up with her. All her hard work on behalf of her family and community, her idyllic and quiet life, had failed to balance her account in the cosmic ledger book. What Sarah thought was her chance to start over now evaporated in the noon day sun, and she realized there was no escaping her debt of negative karma. She had accumulated a disproportionate share of negative karma and there was no cosmic bankruptcy court which could forgive her debt and give her a second chance. Life is not a game of jacks.

Truly deep was the consternation and shock which must have come over all who knew her as this soccer mom when she was unmasked as a one-time member of the notorious Symbionese Liberation Army, Kathleen Soliah, who was wanted for robbery and other crimes, including possibly murder, that occurred over 25 years prior to her arrest. From arrest to trial, she and her family and her friends argued that the length of time that had passed between the crime and her arrest, coupled with her years of lawful and productive living, should be enough to forgive Kathleen for her youthful rebellions. Or at the most she should be just placed on probation.

However, the judge assigned to hear her case was neither impressed nor moved. Kathleen received two consecutive 10-years-to-life terms. A subsequent trial resulted in her receiving an additional six year prison sentence. She is now serving her sentences in a California women's facility.[25]

In Kathleen's case, the Beatles were wrong. Instant karma did not get her. Her karma caught up with her when she thought her game of jacks had turned into the game of life, and she had been granted overs. Kathleen, like so many others, failed to realize that there can be no forgiveness without repentance, and there can be no repentance without restoration. These are not just religious concepts—they are the immutable laws of karma. They are the unbreakable laws of the universe.

When one commits a wrong against another, saying "I'm sorry" is just the beginning of the process. One must turn from one's offending way and restore the offended person to as close to his or her original position as possible. If one has profited from the offense then one must divest oneself of that profit. This is the way of karma.

This law is evident in the 12-Step Program of Alcoholics Anonymous, where steps eight and nine require the making of amends. It is further evidenced in African and Asian spirituality, where being out of a right relationship with a deceased relative can wreak havoc in one's life. In the discipline of psychotherapy, many a therapist has found that the patient's dysfunctions are caused by unresolved issues with another person. These are all examples of the vitality and certainty of karma.

It is no wonder, then, that so many with so much are so miserable. One thinks that one can adjust the ledger book through the acquisition of things. However, one soon discovers that those things are weighing one down, and now one is twice as miserable as before. All too often we grieve the death of one who seemed to have everything but peace of mind. So many times we find ourselves lamenting yet another Richard Cory who confounded our admiration by putting a gun to his head and pulling the trigger.

A word of caution is in order. Do not think that one can seek a veto or suspension of the law of karma in religion. As was set forth above, many of the world's religions have incorporated the law of karma, though it may be called by various names: "reap what you sow"[26]; the "law of laws."[27] Further, do not think for a moment that karma applies only to those who commit criminal offenses. There are many more wanted persons than appear on the nightly news and America's Most Wanted. One can incur karma by having negative thoughts just as quickly as one can by committing wrong acts or saying hurtful words.

Karma is the driving force behind so many who go insane because of the needle pricks to their conscience. Karma is the power behind the conscience. And even where one has imprisoned the conscience beneath the murky waters of the id, karma continues to chip away at the soul until one collapses to the ground for lack of support of the body.

Karma is also the power that elevates people above chance and circumstance and balances the scale tilted by nature and nurture. Karma is the reason that kings are toppled and paupers are crowned. Karma is the cause of the still born delivery of the queen, and karma causes a world renowned classical pianist and composer to be born of the rape of an impoverished and powerless young lady.

As we have said earlier, we cannot overcome the force of karma. We can not overcome karma or suspend its operation by appealing to religion or magic; nor can we exert our mind and will over it as Bruce Lee imagined he could through martial arts in his enlightening work, "The Tao of Jeet Kune Do." As the tragedy of Bruce Lee's death dramatizes all too well, all we can do is to submit to this immoveable law of the universe or be crushed by it.

It is in the hope that we will submit to the reality of karma that this path is revealed. We have set forth in this work 21 rules that will enable us all to play the game of life more authentically and to win at the game.

All that is asked is that those who read this work give it a try. Is it not time that for once in your life you are willing to come out of the darkness and to walk in the light? Let go of mediocrity and ascend the heights of karma so you will be able to soar among the stars without ever leaving the earth.

You have tried everything else and you have failed. Your life is a wreck. Your ball is lodged against a tree and the more you hit it the deeper it falls into the foliage. That is because karma is a self executing law that governs the game of life. The more you swing the worst your life becomes and it will become more out of control unless you play it where it lies. Stop swinging and realize you must pay a penalty for past misdeeds. That is an acceptable loss. Remember, sometimes the best drivers have to back up to go forward.

You are at the beginning of a marvelous game that will be far more lively and enjoyable and which will lead you to victory. All you have to do is learn to play it where it lies.

Notes

1. I implore my readers to accept this statement in the spirit in which it is offered—a statement of fact and not one of derision.

2. Wilken, Robert Louis, "Porphyry The Most Learned Critic of All," chap. In *The Christians as the Romans Saw Them*, 2d ed., Yale Univ. Press: New Haven, 2003, 132-33.

3. I cite these examples without offering any comment as to whether or not those philosophical infusions were "good" or "bad." Many have argued that Paul was the worst thing that ever happened to Christianity and some have said that Qutb is responsible for the wave of Islamic terrorism that afflicts the world today. Whether there is any merit to these arguments I take no position on at this juncture, except to point out that the existence of these arguments prove my premise of the transformative power of philosophy and that is the only point I wish to make here.

4. Romans 7:15-23, KJV.

5. Ephesians 6:11-12, KJV.

6. I have argued elsewhere how Christians can go about discerning these rules. See my recently published work, *What Must I Do? Bridging the Gap Between Being and Doing*, Kendall/Hunt (2006).

7. I use this term instead of cross-cultural to denote an actual blending of cultures such as McDonald's, an American icon, in the Philippines serving both American and Filipino dishes.

8. Luke 20:9-18; Matthew 21:33-46; Mark 12: 1-12; Cf. Isaiah 5:1-7.

9. Philippians 4:13, KJV.

10. 1 John 4:4, KJV.

11. Professor D.Z. Phillips has written an engaging book on this theme entitled, *Religion and Friendly Fire: Examining Assumptions in Contemporary Philosophy of Religion*: The Vonhoff Lectures and Seminars, University of Groningen 1999-2000, England: Ashgate Publishing Ltd. (2004)" in which he argues that certain friends of Christianity have inflicted serious damage on the religion and how others perceive it.

12. Robert Markus, "Augustine: a defence of Christian mediocrity," in *The End of Ancient Christianity* (Cambridge University Press, 1993, 1990), 45.

13. Mark: 7:15, KJV. One should read the entire chapter to get a full understanding of this point.

14. Ecc. 1:9, KJV.

15. Lord Russell of Liverpool, "No Corpse, No Crime," in *Though the Heavens Fall* (London: Cassell & Co., Ltd., 1916), 112-113.

16. Ibid., 113.

17. This story was well reported by national news outlets and my rendition of it is based on many of those reports as well as my conversations with people closer to the events and my watching her trial via Court TV.

18. *II Corinthians* 12:2.

19. I received this story in a slightly different version from one of my Internet correspondents in January 1999. I regret to say that the name of the correspondent and the source of the story have been lost.

20. We must be careful not to underestimate the epistemological problems occasioned by this event. Can we know something if it is incorrect? I knew that I had my wallet at lunch. It turned out that I was in error. Is there then any sense in which I can talk about knowing that I had my wallet? If a matter is erroneous, can one know it? Or, is anything short of accuracy and truth knowledge at all? What then do we call my knowledge of my wallet? Faith? Belief? Keep in mind that I did not think I knew where my wallet was, I knew exactly where it was. We shall have to explore these matters at another place.

21. Yes, this is the former wife of whom I spoke earlier.

22. I have modified the riddle by adding the last phrase regarding night.

23. http://www.transcendentalists.com/success.htm (Retrieved April 29, 2006).

24. Percy Bysshe Shelley (1792-1822), http://www.potw.org/archive/potw 46.html (Accessed May 16, 2006).

25. http://www.fact-index.com/k/ka/kathleen_soliah.html (Retrieved May 4, 2006).

26. *Galatians* 6:7.

27. Ralph Waldo Emerson, "Divinity School Address," http:// www.emersoncentral.com/divaddr.htm (Retrieved April 29, 2006).

28. This story was well reported by national news outlets and my rendition of it is based on many of those reports as well as my conversations with people closer to the events and my watching her trial via Court TV. 18 II Corinthians 12:2.

29. I received this story in a slightly different version from one of my Internet correspondents in January 1999. I regret to say that the name of the correspondent and the source of the story have been lost.

30. We must be careful not to underestimate the epistemological problems occasioned by this event. Can we know something if it is incorrect? I knew that I had my wallet at lunch. It turned out that I was in error. Is there then any sense in which I can talk about knowing that I had my wallet? If a matter is erroneous, can one know it? Or, is anything short of accuracy and truth knowledge at all? What then do we call my knowledge of my wallet? Faith? Belief? Keep in mind that I did not think I knew where my wallet was, I knew exactly where it was. We shall have to explore these matters at another place.

31. Yes, this is the former wife of whom I spoke earlier.

32. I have modified the riddle by adding the last phrase regarding night.

33. http://www.transcendentalists.com/success.htm (Retrieved April 29, 2006).

34. Percy Bysshe Shelley (1792-1822), http://www.potw.org/archive/ potw46.html (Accessed May 16, 2006).

35. http://www.fact-index.com/k/ka/kathleen_soliah.html (Retrieved May 4, 2006)

36. Galatians 6:7.

37. Ralph Waldo Emerson, "Divinity School Address," http://www. emersoncentral.com/divaddr.htm (Accessed May 8, 2006), 3.

ABOUT THE AUTHOR

Don E. Peavy, Sr., PhD. Teaches religious studies at California State University at Long Beach and Victor Valley College as well as philosophy, ethics, and religion at the University of Phoenix, Southern California Division. He also teaches theology and divinity courses via the Internet for Canyon College.

Prior to moving to Southern California, Dr. Peavy practiced law in Fort Worth, Texas, his hometown. He left the practice of law to enter active ministry. He graduated from Brite Divinity School at Texas Christian University and attained his PhD in religious studies from Hamilton University. He is busy at work on a second PhD. from Claremont Graduate University in theology, ethics, and culture. Until recently, Dr. Peavy served as the pastor of McCarty Memorial Christian Church (Disciples of Christ) in Los Angeles, California.

He is the author of several novels as well as a book on Christian ethics entitled, "What Must I Do?": Bridging the Gap Between Being and Doing, which was published by Kendall/Hunt in 2006.